EAR-TRAINING AND
SIGHT-SINGING

Applied to Elementary Musical Theory

EAR-TRAINING AND
SIGHT-SINGING

Applied to Elementary Musical Theory

A Practical and Coördinated Course
For Schools and Private Study

By

GEORGE A. WEDGE

SCHIRMER BOOKS
A Division of Macmillan Publishing Co., Inc.
NEW YORK

COLLIER MACMILLAN PUBLISHERS
LONDON

SCHIRMER BOOKS
A Division of Macmillan Publishing Co., Inc.
866 Third Avenue, New York, N.Y. 10022

Collier Macmillan Canada, Ltd.

Printed in the United States of America

printing number
8   9   10

ANALYTICAL TABLE OF CONTENTS

TABLE OF CONTENTS

PREFACE

The purpose of this book is to present the Elements of Music in a direct and concise manner; to show as simply as possible the reason for these things; to give the pupil material for practice and instruct him how to use this material.

Each step is presented in three ways: first, exercises to be written; second, exercises for dictation to be used in Ear-training; third, exercises for Sight-reading.

Section A of each Lesson contains the exercises for written work; Sections B and C the exercises for Ear-training and Sight-reading.

In class-work it has been found practical to use three fifty-minute periods a week, devoting a period to each Section.

Following is the plan of the book, showing the development of the work and the order in which the factors are taken up.

AN ACKNOWLEDGEMENT

The author wishes to express his thanks to Dr. Frank Damrosch for his confidence in this work and his generous attitude as it was developed in the classes at the Institute of Musical Art;—

To Miss Helen W. Whiley, whose coöperation and enthusiasm in presenting this subject have made the work possible; also, for writing the exercises for study of the first fifteen lessons in Ear-training;—

To Dr. Thomas Tapper for reviewing the manuscript and for valuable suggestions in the arrangement of the material;—and

To Dr. Percy Goetchius' excellent book, "Melody-Writing," for the order of presentation of the points in Melodic Construction.

GEORGE A. WEDGE.

EAR-TRAINING AND SIGHT-SINGING

Applied to Elementary Musical Theory

EAR-TRAINING AND SIGHT-SINGING

CHAPTER I

General Definitions

Music is an Art, the medium of which is Sound.

All art-forms, such as painting, sculpture, architecture and dancing, are means of self-expression. They differ in the medium of expression. The painter uses lines and color; the musician uses sound.

Musical Sound or **Tone** differs from noise in that it has a regular and fixed number of vibrations per second. Tone possesses four properties—Pitch, Duration, Quality and Quantity. Noise is generally lacking in one or more of these properties. There are certain noises which, by their constant repetition, approximate sound; such as those made by a motor or trolley car when speeding up.

The *Pitch* of a sound is determined by the number of vibrations per second. The greater the number of vibrations, the higher the pitch: the fewer, the lower the pitch. If we stretch a rubber band and use a ruler as a movable bridge, we are able, by plucking the band, to make sounds of different pitches. The greater the distance from the ruler to the fixed end of the band, the slower the vibrations and the lower the pitch; the shorter the distance, the faster the vibrations and the higher the pitch. In a piano the longer strings produce the lower sounds.

The *Duration* of a sound is the length of time the vibrations continue.

The *Quality* or *Color* of a sound is determined by the instrument which produces the sound. It is quality which tells us whether the tone is that of a voice, violin or piano.

The *Quantity* of a sound is determined by the volume; if it is loud or soft.

Musical tones are represented upon paper by *Notes*. The notes are placed upon five parallel, equidistant, horizontal lines, called a *Staff*. Each line and space represents a definite pitch assigned to it by a key-letter called a *Clef*, placed at the beginning of the staff. Only two clefs are commonly used, the G and F.

1

The *G-Clef*, which was originally a Gothic letter G, is always so placed as to circle around the second line,  which determines the pitch of that line to be G; the next space above is A; the next line above is B; etc. The space below G is F, the line below that is E, etc. Each successive line and space is named in alphabetic order until the eighth degree is reached. This is a duplication of the first sound and has the same name.

The *F-Clef*, which was a Gothic letter F, is placed with its two dots on either side of the fourth line of the staff. This determines the pitch of that line to be F; the next space above is G, the next line is A, etc. The space below F is E, the next line 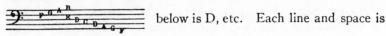 below is D, etc. Each line and space is named in alphabetic order until the eighth is reached.

In piano music there are two *Staves* used together, with the *G-Clef* on the upper, which is commonly called the treble staff, and the *F-Clef* on the lower, commonly called the bass staff. This is really one large staff of eleven lines with the middle line omitted.

 The eleven-line staff was known as the *Great Staff*.

The great staff was originally invented to accommodate the tones for the four voices—soprano, alto, tenor and bass. The center line had the pitch C which all the voices could sing, and the lines above and below included the sounds within the range of the voices. The eleven lines as a unit group were difficult to read: therefore the middle line, C, was later omitted, leaving five lines above and below.

Music requires the use of tones higher and lower in pitch than the degrees of the staff. We extend the staff for these pitches by the use of lines known as *Leger-Lines:*

For convenience in determining the location or register of tones and in learning the names of the lines and spaces, we divide the Great Staff into octave groups, thus:

C D E F G A B   c d e f g a b   c¹ d¹ e¹ f¹ g¹ a¹ b¹   c² d² e² f² g² a² b²   c³ d³ e³ f³ g³ a³ b³
Great Octave   Small Octave   One-line Octave   Two-line Octave   Three-line Octave

LESSON 1

Section A.

Suggestions for Study:

(1) Make a Great Staff by drawing a dotted line between the treble and bass. Place the following pitches:

c^1, C, c, c^2, c^3, G, g^1, g^2, g, g^3, d, d^2, D, d^1, d^3, a^2, A, a, a^1, E, e^2, e, e^1, e^3, b, b^1, b^2, B, f^2, f, F, f^1.

Example:

(2) After the pitches are written, recite the name and register of each without reference to the table.

(3) Place pencil on a line or space and quickly name the pitch and register.

(4) Place the following pitches in the treble: A, C, F, B, E, D, G.

(5) Place the following pitches in the bass: D, B, E, C, A, G, F.

Section B.

Play c^1 on the piano. Play c^2 and listen to its relation to c^1 in direction and distance. Name the staff position of c^2 (third space, G-clef). Play c^1 and then c. What is the relation in direction and distance? Name the staff position of c. Study c^3 and C in the same way.

Play c. Think the pitch of c^1, sing it; play it on the piano to test your accuracy.

Play c^2. Think and sing c^1.

Play C. Think and sing c^1.

Think the c occurring between C and c^1. Play it on the piano to test your accuracy.

Play c³.   Think and sing c¹.   Think the c occurring between c³ and c¹.   Test with the piano.

Play c¹			Play c¹		
" C	} think c².		" C	}	think c₁
" c			" c²		
" c³			" c³		

Sing c¹; think c², test on the piano; place on the staff.

"	c	"
"	c³	"
"	C	"

Sing g¹; think g, test on the piano; place on the staff.

"	g²	"
"	g³	"
"	G	"

Sing f¹; think F, test on the piano; place on the staff.

"	f²	"
"	f³	"
"	f	"

Section C.

The following exercises are to be sung when in the vocal range; otherwise they are to be mentally determined and tested.

Play c¹ first each time; think   c² – c¹   c² – c³
                                 c – c¹   c¹ – c³
Place each on the staff.   c – c²   c³ – c
                                 c – C   c² – C
                                 C – c¹   C – c³
                                 C – c²

Play c² first each time; think   c² – c¹   c² – c³
                                 c – c¹   c¹ – c³
Place each on the staff.   c – c²   c³ – c
                                 c – C   c² – C
                                 C – c¹   C – c³
                                 C – c²

Play g¹ first each time; think   g¹ – g²
                                 g¹ – g
   Place each on the staff.   g¹ – G
                                 g¹ – g³

Play e^1 first each time; think $e^1 - e^2$
$\qquad\qquad\qquad\qquad\qquad\qquad e^1 - e$
$\qquad$ Place each on the staff. $\quad e^1 - E$
$\qquad\qquad\qquad\qquad\qquad\qquad e^1 - e^3$

Play c^1 first each time; think $C - c^1 - c^2 \qquad c - C - c^1$
$\qquad\qquad\qquad\qquad\qquad\quad c^1 - c \ - C \qquad c^2 - c^3 - c^1$
$\qquad$ Place each on the staff. $\ c^2 - c^1 - c \qquad c^3 - c^1 - c^2$
$\qquad\qquad\qquad\qquad\qquad\quad c^3 - c^2 - c \qquad C - c^1 - c^3$
$\qquad\qquad\qquad\qquad\qquad\quad C - c \ - c^1 \qquad c^2 - c \ - C$
$\qquad\qquad\qquad\qquad\qquad\quad c^1 - C - c \qquad c^2 - c \ - c^1$

Play g^1 first each time; think $g^1 - g^2 - g^3 \qquad g - G - g^1$
$\qquad\qquad\qquad\qquad\qquad\quad g^1 - g \ - G \qquad g^2 - g^3 - g^1$
$\qquad$ Place each on the staff. $\ g^2 - g^1 - g \qquad g^3 - g^1 - g^2$
$\qquad\qquad\qquad\qquad\qquad\quad g^3 - g^2 - g^1 \qquad G - g^1 - g^3$
$\qquad\qquad\qquad\qquad\qquad\quad G - g \ - g^1 \qquad g^2 - g \ - G$
$\qquad\qquad\qquad\qquad\qquad\quad g^1 - G - g \qquad g^2 - g \ - g^1$

Play e^1 first each time; think $e^1 - e^2 - e^3 \qquad e - E - e^1$
$\qquad\qquad\qquad\qquad\qquad\quad e^1 - e \ - E \qquad e^2 - e^3 - e^1$
$\qquad$ Place each on the staff. $\ e^2 - e^1 - e \qquad e^3 - e^1 - e^2$
$\qquad\qquad\qquad\qquad\qquad\quad e^3 - e^2 - e^1 \qquad e^2 - e \ - E$
$\qquad\qquad\qquad\qquad\qquad\quad E - e \ - e^1 \qquad e^2 - e \ - e^1$
$\qquad\qquad\qquad\qquad\qquad\quad e^1 - E - e \qquad E - e^1 - e^3$

Play f^1 first each time; think $F - f^1 - f^2$
$\qquad\qquad\qquad\qquad\qquad\quad f^1 - f \ - F$
$\qquad$ Place each on the staff. $\ f^2 - f^1 - f$
$\qquad\qquad\qquad\qquad\qquad\quad f^3 - f^2 - f^1$

Play d^1 first each time; think $D - d^1 - d^2$
$\qquad\qquad\qquad\qquad\qquad\quad d^1 - d - D$
$\qquad$ Place each on the staff. $\ d^2 - d^1 - d$
$\qquad\qquad\qquad\qquad\qquad\quad d^3 - d^2 - d^1$ (etc.)

Place a^1 first each time; think $A - a^1 - a^2$
$\qquad\qquad\qquad\qquad\qquad\quad a^1 - a \ - A$
$\qquad$ Place each on the staff. $a^2 - a^1 - a$
$\qquad\qquad\qquad\qquad\qquad\quad a^3 - a^2 - a^1$ (etc.)

Play b^1 first each time; think $B - b^1 - b^2$
$\qquad\qquad\qquad\qquad\qquad\quad b^1 - b \ - B$
$\qquad$ Place each on the staff. $b^2 - b^1 - b$
$\qquad\qquad\qquad\qquad\qquad\quad b^3 - b^2 - b^1$ (etc.)

CHAPTER II

Measurements of Distances

In measuring distance with a rule, we count from zero. In music, when measuring the distance on the staff from one note to another, the first note is counted as one and each line and space up to the next note as a degree. This is necessary, because each tone is one of the series of seven pitches. To find the distance between E on the first line of the treble and B on the third line, E is one; F in the next space is two; G on the next line is three; A in the next space is four; and B on the third line is five.

The clock-face is divided into five-minute periods so that exactness in time may be the more readily determined. For the same reason we learn the relative position on the staff of the third, fifth and eighth tones from a line and a space.

If a note is on a line, the third is on the next line.
If a note is in a space, the third is in the next space.
If a note is on a line, the fifth is on the second line.
If a note is in a space, the fifth is in the second space.
If a note is on a line, the eighth is in the fourth space.
If a note is in a space, the eighth is on the fourth line.

If the position of the third, fifth and eighth tones is known, it is easy to place the second, fourth, sixth and seventh tones.

LESSON 2

Section A.

Suggestions for Study:

(1) Write the 8th, 3rd and 5th degrees on the treble or G-staff from C, G, A, E, B and F.

(2) Write the 8th, 3rd and 5th degrees on the bass or F-staff from B, D, F, G, E, A and C.

(3) Write the 8th, 3rd and 5th degrees on the Great Staff from A, c^1, g^2, b, f^1, d, a^1.

NOTE. This is for drill in spacing, i. e., to learn to use the lines and spaces of the staff so that when a note is on the first line we shall know that the third is on the next line, the fifth on the second line and the eighth in the fourth space. The question of the kind of third and fifth, as in scale and interval relation, will be treated later.

(4) Learn the name of the 3rd and 5th degrees from every pitch. From E the third is G; the fifth is B. From D the third is F; the fifth is A; etc.

Section B.

In the foregoing directions the expression "think C" has been used. To think sound means to hear it mentally, to listen to it with the inner ear. Most of us can think the tune America without actually singing it, just as we can think the words without actually saying them. To think sound demands concentration; and facility in it requires practice; but it may be acquired and it must be by the serious student. The beginner in ear-training is always tempted to hum the sound he is trying to think. Singing has a vital part to play in training the ear, but only as a guide and not as a final necessity. Use it as a crutch which may be discarded as ability to think sound develops. In practising the work as outlined it may at first be necessary to sing the exercises, but do not neglect constantly to make the effort to think sound.

NOTE. The above does not refer to *Sight-Singing*, which is quite a different matter.

(1) Comparison of a given tone with the 5th tone above it, as C to G.

If c^1 is considered 1, then c^2 is 8 because it is the 8th tone above, and g^1 is similarly the 5th.

Take c^1 as 1.

Play 1 8 1 (c^1 c^2 c^1).

Play 1 8 5 (c^1 c^2 g^1).

Play these two groups several times and compare the effect of each.

1 8 1 is complete and finished. As a contrast, 1 8 5 is unsatisfactory. Stopping on 5, we expect another tone.

Play 1 8 5 8 and observe that the addition of 8 completes and finishes the group.

Play 1 8. Play 1 5 and compare with 1 8. Repeat, and listen to determine the difference of pitch and the difference in distance between the tones.

(2) Play 8 1; 8 5. Play several times and compare.

(3) Listen carefully as you play **1 5 8 5 1**; immediately re-produce the sounds mentally; in other words, think them. Study the following groups in the same way.

1 8 5 1 8; 1 8 5 8 1; 1 5 1 5 1; 1 5 1 5 8; 8 5 8 5 1; 8 5 8 5 8; 8 5 1 8 5 8.

(4) Play 1. Think 8. Think 5. Sing 5. Test on the piano
Play 8. Think 1. Think 5. Sing 5 and test.
Play 5. Think 8. Sing 8 and test.
Play 5. Think 1. Sing 1 and test.

(5) Play **1 5 8**. Note the distance from **1** to **5**. Try to think a sound which may be placed between; find this sound on the piano.

You have probably played the tone e^1, which is the third tone above c^1, and is therefore called 3. Play **1 3 5 8**. Compare this with **1 5 8**. Play each several times. After some study, think the sounds in each group. Which group has the more pleasing sound?

Play	8 5 1	Compare with	8 5 3 1
"	1 8 5 1	"	"	1 8 5 3 1
"	1 5 5 8	"	"	1 3 5 5 8
"	8 5 1 5 8	"	"	8 5 3 1 3 5 8
"	1 5 8 5 1	"	"	1 3 5 8 5 3 1
"	8 5 1 5 8	"	"	8 5 3 1 3 5 8
"	8 1 5 8	"	"	8 1 3 5 8

Note that the addition of 3 to any combination of 1, 5 and 8 softens and beautifies the effect of the whole group by filling in the space between 1 and 5, which alone is hard and hollow.

(6) Study the following groups as indicated:

(a) Play each group. (b) Think it. (c) Write on the staff in both clefs.

1 3 5 8	8 5 3 5 3 5 1	3 1 3 5 8 5 3 1	5 3 5 1 5 3 1
8 5 3 1	1 3 3 5 5 8 1	5 8 5 3 1	5 1 5 3 5 1 5 8
8 5 3 5 8	8 5 5 3 3 1 8	5 3 1 3 5 8	5 1 1 3 3 5 8
8 5 3 5 1	3 5 8 5 3 5	5 3 5 3 1 3 1	
1 3 5 3 1	3 1 3 5 3 5 8	5 8 5 8 5 3 1	
1 3 5 3 5 3 1	3 5 8 5 8 5 1	5 1 5 8 5 3 1	

These groups should be practised daily. Vary the practice by singing the groups instead of playing them, but always think the sound first.

(7) *Exercises in Sight-Singing*, to be practised as follows:

(a) Play 1 3 5 8.

(b) Read exercise through mentally, thinking, first, the number-name and sound, next the letter-name and sound.

(c) Sing, with number and letter-names.

(d) Test with piano.

NOTE. It is most important always to think the sound of the pitches before singing. Use the piano only to test.

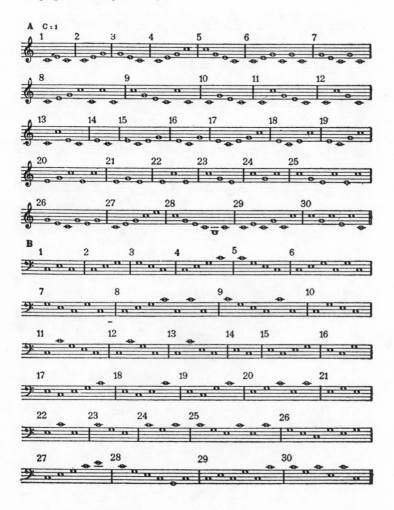

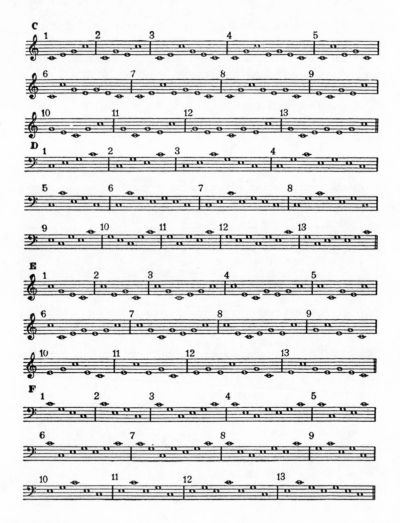

Section C.

(1) These groups should also be practised, using G as 1, in which case B is 3 and D is 5.   Also take F as 1, A as 3 and C as 5.

Play 1.	Think 5.	Sing it.	Test.
" 1.	" 3.	" "	"
" 5.	" 1.	" "	"
" 3.	" 1.	" "	"

Play 5.   Think 3.   Sing it.   Test.
   " 3.   " 5.   " "   "

(2) Take C as 1. Play 1 3 5 8.

Sing a measure or two of the following songs, and any other familiar ones. Decide each time whether the first sound is 1, 3, 5 or 8.

America, Star-Spangled Banner, Annie Laurie, Old Black Joe, Swanee River, Battle Hymn of the Republic, Glory, Glory, Hallelujah, The Marseillaise, Dixie, Yankee Doodle.

    (3) Play 1. Think 1 3 5 8. Think 3. Sing it.   Test it.
      Think 1 3 5 8. Think 5; sing and test.
      "   1 3 5 8.   " 8 "   "   "

Constantly practise this, taking any sound as 1. Think and sing 1 3 5 8. Then 1, 3, 5 and 8, in any order.

An instant recognition of 1 3 5 and 8 is of the utmost importance. In fact, further development is hindered until one has reached some degree of proficiency in this step.

    (4) *Exercises in Sight-Singing.* Practise as outlined in the preceding Lesson.

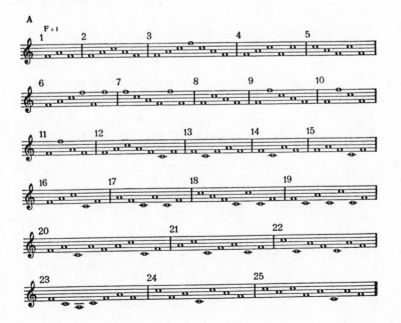

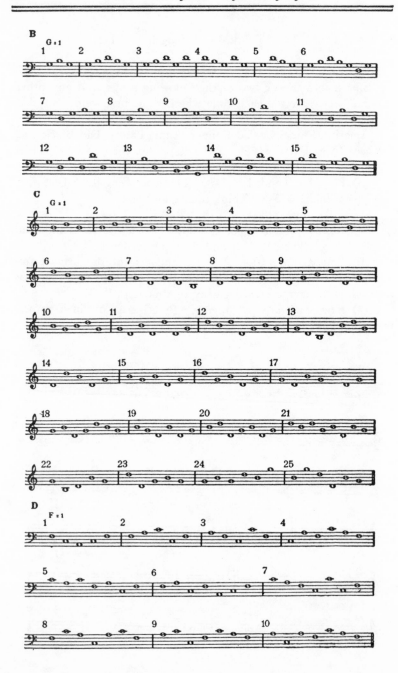

CHAPTER III
Meter and Rhythm

Meter or Time in music is the regular pulsation which is made by a feeling of stress or accent followed by a period of relaxation or non-accent. If we are walking and a band plays we immediately keep time with the pulse of the music.

There are three fundamental meters in music:

Duple, having an accented followed by an unaccented pulse or beat.

Triple, having an accented followed by two unaccented pulses.

Quadruple, having an accented followed by three unaccented pulses.

These three meters correspond somewhat to our breathing. As we breathe, the inhalation corresponds to the unaccented pulse in music, the exhalation to the accented pulse. When exercising, the periods occupied in inhaling and exhaling are of approximately equal duration. This corresponds to duple meter. When we are relaxed or asleep the exhalation is from twice to three times as long as the inhalation. This corresponds to triple or quadruple meter. It will be seen that, in each of these, the breathing begins with the unaccented beat, or up-beat. This accounts for the fact that it is more natural to begin a composition on the up-beat. Music generally ends on an accent.

Though this regular pulsation does not vary, there are tones held longer than the pulse or several tones played upon one pulse. To accomplish this a definite mathematical value must be assigned to each pulse.

Rhythm in music is the arrangement of tones of different value within the meter.

When notes of equal value are used throughout a phrase the rhythm is *Uniform*.

When the value of a note is greater than one pulse, it is known as *Added Beat*.

When the value of a note is less than one pulse, it is known as a *Divided Beat*. Divisions of note-values are generally by two or a multiple of two.

A *triplet* is a group of 3 equal notes of the same value as the one-half subdivision. The numeral 3 is written under the group;

e. g.,

A *quintuplet* is a group of 5 equal notes of the same value as the one-fourth subdivision. The numeral 5 is written under the group; e. g., ♩♪♪♪♪

Modern notation employs the following notes: **o** a whole; ♩ a half; ♩ a quarter; ♪ an eighth; ♪ a sixteenth; ♪ a thirty-second; ♪ a sixty-fourth.. The round part of the note is known as the *head*. The line drawn to the head of the note is the *stem*. The curved line attached to the stem is the *hook*. A straight,

heavy line connecting the stems of notes is called a *beam*: ♫♫♫

To show passage of time in music when there is nothing to be played, we use symbols known as *Rests*, which correspond in value to the notes.

Whole   Half   Quarter   Eighth   Sixteenth   Thirty-second   Sixty-fourth

A *Dot* after a note increases its value one-half; a double dot, three-fourths: ♩. = ♩ ♪   ♩.. = ♩ ♪ ♪

The curved line connecting the heads of two notes of the same pitch, the second of which is not to be restruck, is called

a *Tie*: ♩ ♪

The stressed and relaxed pulses of a meter may be arranged in any order. A *Bar* is drawn across the staff to show the accented pulse of the meter. The group of stressed and relaxed pulses which forms the meter is a *Measure*.

Two figures, placed after the clef at the beginning of the staff, one above the other, indicate the meter and rhythm. The upper figure indicates the meter or the number of pulses in a measure. The lower figure indicates the rhythm or the kind of note which receives a beat. This is the *Metric Signature*, or *Time-signature*.

Thus $\frac{2}{4}$ indicates that there are two beats in each

measure, and that a quarter-note receives one beat.

Half, quarter and eighth-notes are commonly used as units of
Rhythm.   We may have 2/2, 2/4 or 2/8; 3/2, 3/4 or 3/8; 4/2, 4/4
or 4/8.

LESSON 3

Section A.

Suggestions for Study:

(1) Write four measures of 2/2, 2/4, 2/8, making the rhythm
uniform in the first three measures and with an added beat (one
note) in the fourth measure.

(2) Write four measures of 3/2, 3/4, 3/8, making the rhythm
uniform in the first three measures and with an added beat (one
note) in the fourth measure.

Section B.

(1) In training ourselves to determine the meter and hear the
rhythm it is first necessary to maintain an even pulsation or beat.
Count 1–2, 1–2, 1–2, 1–2, and try to keep a steady rate of speed
(tempo).   Walk at a steady tempo, a step to a beat, counting 1–2 as
you do so.   A metronome is invaluable as a test and a help in this
practice, just as the piano is in the practice of pitch.

(2) Tap the beat 1–2, 1–2, with a pencil, using the syllable
la; intone quarter-note values (sing on one pitch).   Tap the beat
and intone half-note values; hold the tone until you have tapped
two beats.

(3) Tap the beat and, using the pitches 1 3 5 8 5 3 1, sing
the note-values of the following exercises:

($\frac{2}{8}$ Two beats in a measure.)

♪ = 1 beat.

CHAPTER IV

Keys and Scales

Tone is a term applied to pitch; for example, the pitch C, or the tone C.

Tone is also applied to the distance from one pitch to the next upon the staff. There are two kinds of tone, the *half-tone* or *semitone* and the *whole tone*.[1] A half-tone is the difference in pitch between sounds made by playing any two adjacent keys on the piano. A whole tone is two half-tones.

If the successive pitches on the staff from G to g[2] are played on the piano, it will be found that they are represented by the white keys of the piano. The only white keys which come together, without black keys between, are E and F, B and C; therefore, the distance on the staff from E to F, and B to C, is a half-tone. The distance between all other successive pitches is a whole tone.

A *Key* is a family of seven related tones. These tones are all derived from one tone, the head of the family, called the *Key-tone*. If a vibrating string gives the pitch C, and we wish to find a tone most nearly related in vibration, but differing in pitch, we would first divide the string into halves and set either half in vibration.

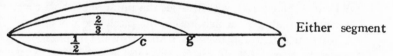 Either segment

vibrates twice as fast and gives the pitch C, one octave higher. Next try dividing the string C into thirds, and set the two-thirds or longer segment into vibration. This gives the pitch G or the fifth tone above C. This fifth tone is the most nearly related tone, differing in pitch, to the fundamental. In the same way the next nearest related tone will be two-thirds of G, or a fifth above G, which is D; the next, a fifth above D, which is A; the

next, a fifth above A, or E; next, a fifth above E, or B.

Conversely, if D is two-thirds of G, and G two-thirds of C, C must be two-thirds of a tone a fifth below, or the tone F. We now have seven different pitches all derived from C, and therefore

[1]Also called half-step and whole-step.

related to C. These pitches constitute the Key of C. C is the Key-tone.

Tones arranged as scale.

When the seven pitches are arranged in the progressive order, C D E F G A B C, they form a *Major Scale*. Numbers are used to designate scale-steps, the key-tone being 1, the next 2, etc., to the eighth tone, which is a duplicate of the first.

The staff is composed of whole tones and half-tones, the half-tones between E and F, B and C. As the Major Scale of C and the pitches of the staff are the same, the major scale must be composed of whole and half-tones, the half-tones between 3 and 4, 7 and 8. The major scale may be constructed from any pitch. If the major scale is constructed from any pitch but C, *accidentals* will have to be used to bring the half-steps in the proper places, as the only half-steps on the staff are between E and F, B and C.

There are five accidentals used:

A Sharp (♯), which raises the pitch one half-tone.

A Flat (♭), which lowers the pitch one half-tone.

A Double Sharp (X), which raises the pitch one whole tone.

A Double Flat (♭♭), which lowers the pitch one whole tone.

A Natural (♮), which restores a note to its staff pitch.

If we start a *major* scale on G, the pitches are G, 1; A, 2; B, 3; C, 4; D, 5; E, 6; F, 7; G, 8.

Now, in a *major* scale, the half-tones must occur between 3 and 4, 7 and 8. There is a half-tone on the staff from B (3) to C (4); but from F (7) to G (8) is a whole tone. Hence, it is necessary to raise the pitch of F to F♯, in order that the half-tone shall fall between 7 and 8.

In the same way, if a scale is constructed from F, the pitches are F, 1; G, 2; A, 3; B, 4; C, 5; D, 6; E, 7; F, 8. In a *major* scale the half-steps must lie between 3 and 4, 7 and 8. From A (3) to B (4) is a whole tone, so the pitch of B must be lowered to B♭. This leaves a whole tone from B♭ (4) to C (5), as is needed from 4 to 5.

There is a half-tone on the staff from E (7) to F (8). The major scale is constructed in the same manner from every pitch.

Besides numbers, names may be applied to the tones of the scale. As scale-tones are tones of a Key-family and are related to the head of the family, or Key-tone, so the members of the family are named as they are related to the head.

The head of the C family is C, and is named the *Tonic*. The eighth tone from the Tonic is the *Octave*. When seeking the different tones of a key, the fifth was found to be the nearest related tone differing in pitch. This is the *Dominant*.

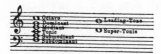

If a tone is placed on the staff midway between C and G, it is E or the third, which is the *Mediant* or middle tone. As C is on the line, the fifth or Dominant is on the second line above; so F, the fourth tone, which is on the second line below, must be the Dominant below, or the *Subdominant*. If A, the sixth tone, is placed midway between the Tonic and Subdominant, it will be the middle tone below, or the *Submediant*. D, the second, the tone above the Tonic, is the *Supertonic* or *Second Dominant*. B, the seventh tone, which progresses into, and seems to prepare, the Tonic, is the *Leading-tone*.

There are two kinds of half-tone progressions:

(1) The half-tone progression from a tone of one letter to a tone of another letter. This is a *Diatonic Half-tone*. E to F is diatonic.

(2) The half-tone progression from one tone to another of the same letter, the pitch having been changed by an accidental. This is a *Chromatic Half-tone*. E to E♭ is chromatic.

Section A.   LESSON 4

Suggestions for Study:

(1) Construct in the treble and bass the Major Scales of C, G, F, D and B♭, using accidentals to establish the whole and half-steps in the proper places.

(2) Write in the treble and bass the following scale-steps in the keys of C, G and F, using accidentals:

1 2 4 3 6 5 7 8
8 7 8 3 5 4 3 2 6 5 7 8 3 2 1
8 5 7 8 6 4 2 3 1 6 5 7 8
1 4 3 2 1 3 5 6 5 7 8 2̲ 3̲ 2̲ 8*

*NOTE. The line under a figure indicates that the scale-step is *above* eight. The line over a figure indicates that the scale-step is *below* one.

(3) Learn the terms applied to scale-steps.

(4) Learn the names of the pitches of 1, 3, 5, 8, of the above keys. (*Example:* The 5th of D is A; the 3rd of B♭ is D; etc.)

(5) Arrange the following pitches in the key of C in four measures, using a half-note as the rhythm; the rhythm uniform for the first three measures; an added beat in the fourth measure; set the proper metric signature after the clef:

1 5 3 4 3 5 8
1 3 5 3 5 8 2̲ 8 7 8

Section B.

(1) Sections of the Scale between 1, 3, 5 and 8. Method of practising the following:

(a) Play 1, 3, 5, 8 from C.
(b) Think the sound of the first group.
(c) Sing it, first by number, next by letter.
(d) Play it as a test of accuracy.
(e) Represent on staff in both clefs.

Repeat this method with each group. Then sing through the entire list, as written, reading from the representation on the staff.

1 2 3 and 3 2 1

1 3	1 2 3 1 3 5 8	1 2 3 3 2 1	1 3 2 1
1 2 3	1 2 3 1 3	1 2 3 5 3 2 1	1 3 2 1 3 5
1 2 3 5	1 2 3 5 3	1 2 3 5 8 5 3 2 1	1 3 2 1 5 1
1 2 3 5 8	1 2 3 5 1		1 3 2 1 5 3 2̲ 1
1 2 3 3 5 5 8	1 2 3 5 3 5 8		1 5 3 2 1
			1 8 3 2 1

3 4 5 and 5 4 3

3 5	3 4 5 8	3 4 5 8 3	3 4 5 5 4 3
3 4 5	3 4 5 1 8	3 4 5 8 5	3 8 5 4 3
3 4 5 3 1	3 4 5 1 3	3 1 3 4 5	5 4 3 5 3
3 4 5 3 8	3 4 5 1 5	3 5 3 4 5	3 5 4 3 5 1
3 4 5 1	3 4 5 8 1	3 8 3 4 5	

5 6 7 8 and 8 7 6 5

5 8	5 6 7 8 1 5	5 6 7 8 8 3 5	5 8 7 6 5	8 7 6 5 3 5
5 6 7 8	5 6 7 8 5	5 6 7 8 5 3 8	5 3 8 7 6 5	8 7 6 5 3 8
5 6 7 8 1	5 8 5 6 7 8	8 3 8 5 6 7 8	5 1 8 7 6 5	8 5 8 7 6 5
5 6 7 8 1 3	5 3 5 6 7 8	5 1 8 5 6 7 8	5 8 7 6 5 3 1	8 3 8 7 6 5
5 6 7 8 3	5 6 7 8 5 3 1	5 1 3 5 6 7 8	8 7 6 5 3 1	8 1 8 7 6 5

These groups should be practised daily, using C, as 1, the first day; F, as 1, the next day; and G, as 1, the day after.

(2) *Exercises in Sight-Singing:*

NOTE. Read exercise mentally before singing.

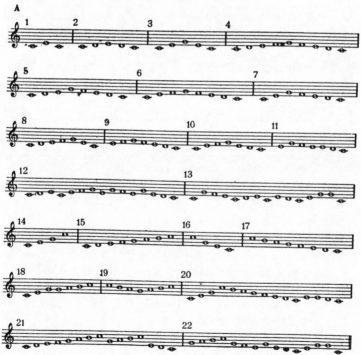

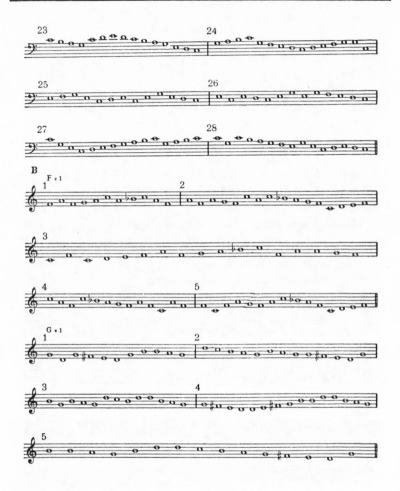

Section C.

(1) After some practice, study the groups of Section B in the following manner, using, for example, 1, 3, 4, 5:

 (a) Sound C on the piano; think and sing 1, 3, 5, 8.

 (b) Think and sing 1, 3, 4, 5, by number and letter-name.

 (c) Sound G; call it 1. Think 1, 3, 5, 8. Think 1, 3, 4, 5; sing and test on piano.

 (d) Sound F; call it 1. Think 1, 3, 5, 8. Think 1, 3, 4, 5; sing, and test on piano.

(2) Practise these groups as follows:
  (a) Sound the key-note.
  (b) Think 1, 3, 5, 8; sing it.
  (c) Recite the numbers of the group; try to think the sounds.
  (d) Sing the numbers; test on piano.
  (e) Recite and sing letter-names.

These groups should also be used for dictation. Have someone help you by playing them on the piano. They should be dictated as follows:

  (f) Play 1, 3, 5, 8.
  (g) Play the group.
  (h) The listener should sing the group in order to memorize it, using the syllable *la;* then he should write down the numbers from memory, and finally place the pitches on the staff; use both clefs.
  (i) Compare what was written with what was played. If there is a mistake, sing the correct and incorrect versions several times until you realize the error.

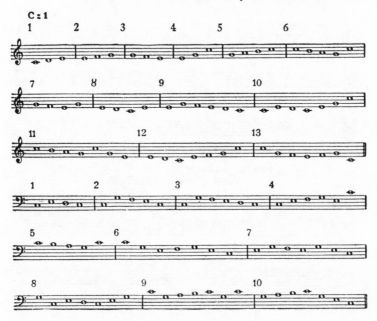

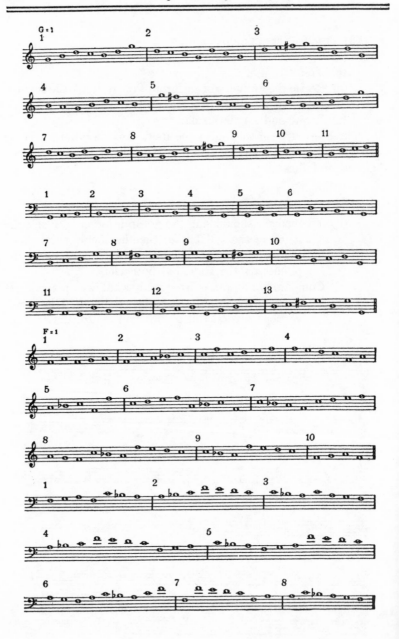

(3) Study 3/4 meter exactly as you studied 2/4.

Count 1, 2, 3; 1, 2, 3; 1, 2, 3; 1, 2, 3, maintaining a steady tempo.

Sing a tone to each beat; also walk a step to each beat.

Sing one tone and tap three beats.   This sound is represented thus: $\mathtt{d.}$

Tap 1, 2, 3, and sing the following:

LESSON 5

Section A.

Suggestions for Study:

(1) Construct the Major Scale in the treble and bass from C♯, D♭, E, E♭, F♯, G♭, A♭, A and B.   Use accidentals to bring the whole and half-steps into their proper places.

(2) Indicate on the staff the following scale-steps in the treble in the keys of D, B♭ and A: 1 5 3 6 5 4 3 5 8 7 8.

(3) Indicate on the staff the following scale-steps in the bass in the keys of E♭, E and A♭: 1 4 3 2 6 5 4 3 5 8 7 8.

(4) Indicate on the staff the following scale-steps in the treble in the keys of B, D♭, F♯: 8 5 7 8 6 4 3 2 5 7̄ 1.

(5) Arrange the following pitches in the key of A Major, in four measures of a quarter-note rhythm, the last measure to be an added beat of one note:

1 3 4 4 3 2 3 2 7̄ 1.
8 5 8 3 5 7̄ 1.

Section B.

(1) Play C. Sing 1 2 3 4 5 6 7 8. Repeat, singing the letters C D E F G A B C. Sing the scale from G, first using numbers, then letters.

What accidental is required? Why? Always name the accidental when you call that tone by its letter-name.

(2) Turn to the groups of numbers on page 20, Lesson 4, Section B, and sing by letter-name, using G as 1. Write in both clefs.

(3) The following exercises are for singing and for practice in dictation:

  (a) Sing by numbers.

  (b) Dictation: 1. Sing the group of tones played on the piano, using *la*, in order to memorize the sound.

    2. Think the numbers.

    3. Write the pitches on the staff in key of G.

    4. After you have written the pitches on the staff, sing them by number.

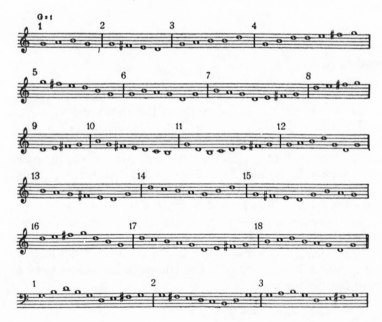

Section C.

(1) The Study of 2/4 with Pitches.

The following exercises are for practice in dictation:

(a) Have someone play the melody several times until you can remember it.

(b) Test your memory of the melody by singing it, using *la*, and tapping the beat.

(c) Analyze the rhythm. Each melody is a phrase. Represent the note-values without pitches. Example:

No. 1 would be represented thus: $\frac{2}{4}$ ♩ ♩ ᛁ ♩ ♩ ᛁ ♩ ♩ ᛁ ♩ ‖

(d) Analyze the pitch. Write the numbers.

(e) Represent on the staff.

Sometimes you can vary this practice by writing the exercise in a different key and note-value, and by writing it on the bass staff.

NOTE. After singing the melody as indicated in Step B, above, make it a habit to *think* sound. Never hum the melody. If your memory of it fails, have it played again.

If you cannot find someone to dictate these melodies to you, memorize them by singing them several times, using *la*. Then proceed as indicated above, analyzing the rhythm and pitch, and representing on the staff.

(2) *Exercises in Sight-Singing:*

CHAPTER V
Key-Signatures

We have found that, in writing music in any key but C, there are tones which must be altered by accidentals in order to produce the correct form of the major scale. Instead of writing the accidentals before these tones each time they recur, they are placed at the beginning of the staff.

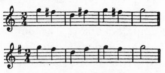

The accidental, or group of accidentals, at the beginning of the staff is called the *Key-Signature*.

The number of sharps or flats denotes the *Key*.

In the series of the major scale tonics constructed on the tones found by dividing the string C into thirds, each new tone is a fifth from the preceding tone. The tones above C are G, D, A, E, B, F♯ and C♯.

The scales built upon these tones as key-tones, require the use of sharps to bring the half-steps into the right place. These are known as *Sharp Keys*. Each new key adds a sharp, which is the seventh step.

The tones found below C are F, B♭, E♭, A♭, D♭ and G♭. Scales built upon these tones as key-tones require flats to bring half-steps into the right place, and are known as *Flat Keys*. Each new key adds a flat, which is the fourth step.

The most comprehensive arrangement of these key-tones is

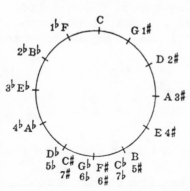

shown upon a clock-face, placing C at twelve o'clock, each new sharp key an hour to the right, and each new flat key an hour to the left. The hour at which the key occurs gives the number of sharps or flats in the signature. A is at three o'clock (halfway), and has three sharps in its sig‑ nature; E♭ is halfway on the other side, and has three flats in its signature.

G♭ and F♯ occur at the same place, also D♭ and C♯, and C♭ and B. If the scale from G♭ and F♯ is played on the piano the same (piano) keys are used. The same is true of D♭ and C♯, C♭ and B. For every flat key there is a sharp key; thus, A♭ is G♯, E♭ is D♯, F is E♯. Conversely, every sharp key has a flat key. In either case there result keys with double-sharps and double-flats. This is found to be impracticable on account of the difficulty in reading. Compositions are seldom written in G♭ or C♯ major.

The accidentals used in a key-signature are arranged in the order in which they occur as the new keys are constructed. Each accidental is placed a little to the right of the preceding accidental and in a definite position on the staff. The first sharp key is G, adding F♯, which is placed on the fifth line of the treble and fourth line of the bass; the next key is D, adding C♯, placed in the third space of treble and second space of bass; the next key is A, adding G♯, placed in the space above treble and fourth space of bass. Each succeeding key adds a sharp. The sharps are arranged as in the illustration.

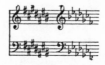

The first flat key is F, adding B♭, which is placed on the third line of the treble and second line of the bass; next B♭, adding E♭, etc. The flats are arranged as in the illustration.

It is necessary to learn the names and number of sharps or flats in the key-signatures. To tell the key from the signatures, the last sharp in the signature is the seventh of the key. If the last sharp is A♯, the key is B. The name of the next to the last flat in the signature is the name of the key.

LESSON 6

Section A.

Suggestions for Study:

(1) Write in the treble and bass the 1, 3, 5, 8 of all major scales, using signatures.

(2) Study the position of the keys upon the clock-face; then, looking at the clock, recite the keys in order. Name keys, jumping

to different hours.   In this way the number of sharps or flats in the signature will become familiar.

(3) Learn to recite the sharps in the order in which they occur: F♯, C♯, G♯, D♯, A♯, E♯ and B♯.

Learn to recite the flats: B♭, E♭, A♭, D♭, G♭, C♭ and F♭.

(4) Learn to determine quickly the key from the signature. Make each sharp the last of a signature and recite the pitch one half-tone higher, as: F♯, G; C♯, D; etc.

Section B.

(1) Review exercises of Lesson 2, Sections B and C, page 8, also Lesson 4, Sections B and C, page 20, singing numbers and letters, using C, F and G as 1.

(2) The following exercises are for singing and dictation:

    (a) Sing by numbers and letters.

(3) Dictation:

    (a) Sing the group of tones played on the piano.

    (b) Think the tones and numbers.

    (c) Write the pitches on the staff.

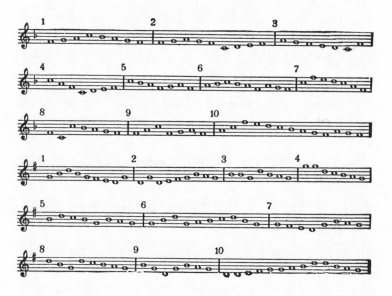

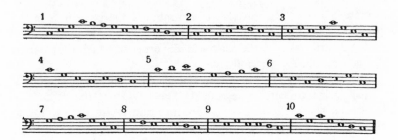

Section C.

(1) Study of 3/4 with pitches.

The following exercises are for practice in dictation. Work according to directions given in Lesson 5, Section C, page 27.

(2) *Exercises in Sight-Singing:*

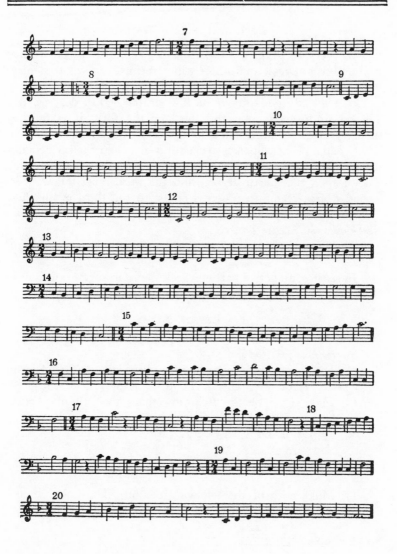

CHAPTER VI

Rest and Active Tones

In every scale there are certain degrees upon which we may stop and feel at rest, and others which seem to the ear to demand progression or resolution.

If a melody ends upon the first or the eighth degrees, it is finished; if it ends upon the third or the fifth, it is finished, though giving the impression of an upward or questioning inflection. Try to end a melody upon the seventh degree, and the ear demands that the eighth follow; upon the sixth degree, and the fifth must follow; upon the fourth degree, and the third must follow. The second degree seems to progress either to the third or the first.

The tones 1, 3, 5 and 8, upon which a melody may end, are *Rest Tones* or *Inactive Tones*.

The tones 2, 4, 6 and 7, which demand resolution, are *Active Tones*.

In science, all active particles seek the nearest rest. In music, all *Active Tones* seek, or resolve to, the nearest *Rest Tones*.

LESSON 7

Section A.

Suggestions for Study:

(1) Learn the Rest Tones in every key, i. e., 1, 3, 5, 8, from every pitch. Example: D, F♯, A and D; E♭, G, B♭, E♭.

(2) Make each of the following tones the 7th of a scale; resolve them, and name the key to which each belongs: B, G♯, D♯, F♯, A♯, C♯, E♯, E, D, A, C, G, F, B♯.

Example:

(3) Make each of the following the 6th of a scale; resolve, and name key: A, E♭, E, B♭, F♯, C, B, F, C♯, G, D♯, G♯, D, A♭.

Example:

(4) Make each of the following the 4th of a scale; resolve, and name key: F, D, G, C, A♭, C♭, A, E, E♭, G♭, B, D♭, B♭, F♭.

Example:

[34]

Section B.

(1) Activity and Rest: Study of the 7th Step.

Play 1 3 5 8.

Play 1 3 5 8 7.

Compare the effect of the first with the second. The first is final or satisfying in its effect. The second is the opposite. When we pause on 7 we feel that it must go to 8.

1 3 5 and 8 represent rest. Any other tone is active and must progress (resolve) to one of the rest tones. Play the following, pausing on 7, and then carry it forward to where you feel it should go:

8 7; 1 2 3 2 1 $\bar{7}$; 5 3 1 $\bar{7}$; 5 8 7.

You may always recognize 7 by its strong tendency to resolve to 8.

(2) Study of the 2nd Step.

Play 5 3 1.

Play 5 3 2. If you pause on 2 you will feel its tendency to go down to 1.

Play 5 3 2 1.

Play 5 3 2 3. This also is a possibility, as 2 may go to either 1 or 3, because both 1 and 3 are rest tones. However, 2 is most easily recognized by its downward tendency to 1.

(3) (*a*) Sing the following. (*b*) Place on the staff, treble and bass clefs, in C, F, G. (These tones on staff may be referred to later and sung by number and letter.)

```
1 5̄ 1           1 3 2 1 7̄ 1    1 5 4 3 2 1 7̄ 1   1 3 2 1        1 5 3 8 3 2 1
1 7̄ 1           1 3 2 3 1 5̄ 1  1 3 5 8 1 7̄ 1     1 3 2 3        1 5 3 2 3 2 1
1 3 5 1 5̄ 1     1 3 2 3 1 7̄ 1  1 8 1 7̄ 1         1 3 5 3 2 3    1 8 3 1 3 2 1
1 3 1 7̄ 1       1 3 5 5̄ 1      1 5 1 7̄ 1         1 3 5 8 3 2 3  1 8 3 5 3 2 3
1 3 2 1 5̄ 1     1 3 5 7̄ 1      1 3 1 7̄ 1         1 5 3 2 3 5 8

3 2 1 5̄ 1       3 1 7̄ 1        3 5 1 7̄ 1         3 8 3 5̄ 1 7̄ 1   3 5 5̄ 1 7̄ 1
3 2 1 7̄ 1       3 1 5̄ 1        3 5 1 5̄ 1         3 8 5 5̄ 5 7̄ 1   3 5 8 1 7̄ 1

5 3 1 5̄ 1       5 1 3 1 5̄ 1    5 3 8 1 7̄ 1       5 8 1 3 5
5 3 1 7̄ 1       5 1 3 1 7̄ 1    5 1 7̄ 1 8 1       5 7̄ 1 2 3
5 1 7̄ 1         5 8 1 7̄ 1      5 7̄ 1 3 5         5 7̄ 1
```

3 2 3 2 1   3 2 1 2 3 2 3 3 1 3 2 3 5 8   3 5 3 2 1 2 1
3 1 2 3 1   3 2 3 5 8   3 5 3 2 3 8 3   3 8 3 2 3 5 1
3 2 3 5 1   3 5 8 3 2 3   3 1 2 1 2 3 1   3 2 1 2 1 5 8
3 2 3 5 3   3 2 1 2 1 2 3

5 3 2 3 1   5 8 3 5 3 2 3 5 8 1 3 1   5 1 3 1 3 2 3   5 8 3̲ 2̲ 8
5 3 2 1   5 3 1 2 1   5 1 2 1 3 2 1 5 8 1 2 1 2 3   5 8 3̲ 2̲ 3̲
5 3 2 3 5 8 5 8 1 2 1   5 8 3 5 3 2 1 5 8 2̲ 8 5 8 2̲ 3̲

1 3 2 1 7̄ 1   5 8 2̲ 8 7 8   3 5 8 2̲ 8 5 8   5 8 7 8
3 1 2 1 7̄ 1 2 1   5 8 3̲ 2̲ 8 7 8 3 5 8 3̲ 8 5 8   8 1 2 1
1 3 5 3 2 1 7̄ 1   5 1 2 1 5 7̄ 1 3 5 8 3̲ 2̲ 8 7 8 8 1 7̄ 1
1 5̄ 1 7̄ 1 2 1   3 1 2 3 1 7̄ 1 5 1 5 7̄ 1 2 1   5 3 2 3 1 7̄ 1
3 5 3 2 3 1 7̄ 1   5 7̄ 1 2 1 5 8 2̲ 8 5 3 1 2 3 5 1

(4) The following should be studied in two ways:
    (a) Sing by number and letter; then with *la;* memorize;
         then write in another key.
    (b) Dictated; sung with *la;* sung by number and letter;
         represented on the staff in C, F or G.

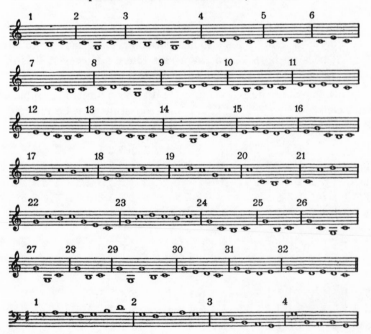

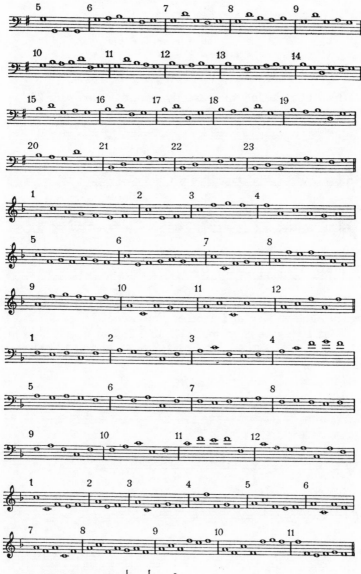

(5) The Study of ♩ ♩ in $\frac{3}{4}$.

(a) Tap the beat.
(b) Sing the rhythm.

(6) Study the following exactly as outlined on page 27.

It is also good practice to rewrite each exercise, after memorizing, in another Key and another time-value.

Thus 1 may be rewritten in G, in 3/2; 2 in C, 3/8; 3 in F, in 3/8; 4 in F, in 3/2; 5 in C, in 3/2; 6 in C, in 3/8; 7 in G, in 3/4; 8 in G, in 3/2.

(7) *Exercises in Sight-Singing:*

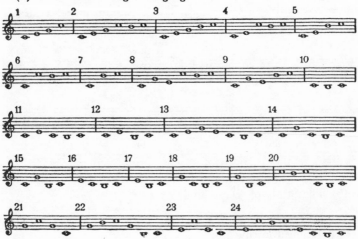

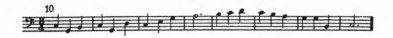

Section C.

(1) Study of 6 and 4 as Active Tones

    (a) Play 1 3 5 3 1.

        Play 1 6. Pausing on 6, you will feel the tendency
to resolve to 5.

        Play 1 6 5 and feel the activity coming to rest; 6 may al-
ways be recognized by its downward tendency to 5.

    (b) Sing the following, always pausing on 6 to feel its
activity:

1 3 5 6 5	3 5 6 5	5 6 5 8	5 6 5 1	1 6 5 $\bar{7}$ 1
1 5 6 5	3 8 5 6 5	5 8 5 6 5	5 8 7 8 5 6 5	
1 6 5 3 1	3 1 5 6 5	5 3 5 6 5	3 5 6 5 3 2 1	
1 6 5 4 3 2 1	3 1 6 5	5 6 5 $\bar{7}$ 1	3 5 6 5 3 2 3	
1 6 5 8	3 5 1 3 5 6 5	5 6 5 8 $\underline{2}$ 8	1 6 5 3 1 2 1	

    (c) Play 1 2 3 2 1.

        Play 1 4. Pausing on 4, you will feel its downward
tendency toward 3.

1 3 1	1 3 4 3 1 4 3	8 3 4 3 2 1	5 1 2 3 4 3	5 8 5 4 3
1 3 4 3	1 4 3 1 $\bar{7}$ 1	8 5 3 4 3	5 1 4 3	5 8 7 8 3 4 3
1 4 3 2 1	1 4 3 1 2 1	8 5 3 5 3 4 3	5 $\bar{7}$ 1 3 1	5 1 4 3 2 1
1 4 3 1	1 5 3 1 4 3	8 3 4 3	5 $\bar{7}$ 1 4 3	5 3 4 3 2 3
1 5 3 4 3	1 4 3 5 8 $\underline{2}$ 8	8 3 5 3 4 3	5 1 2 1 3 4 3 5 $\bar{7}$ 1 4 3	
		8 3 4 3 2 1	5 1 2 1 4 3	5 3 8 3 4 3

    (d) Sing 4 and 6 in same groups:

1 4 3 1	8 3 4 3 5 6 5	5 4 3 5 6 5 8	3 1 6 5 1 4 3
1 6 5 3 1	$\overline{5}$ 1 4 3 6 5	5 1 4 3 1 6 5	3 2 3 4 3
1 3 4 3 5 6 5	5 $\bar{7}$ 1 4 3 5 6 5	8 1 6 5 1 4 3	
1 4 3 1 6 5			

We have now completed a detailed study of each of the active
tones. One, the 7th step, has a decided and very strong activity
upward to 8.

The other three active tones all have a downward tendency
to 1, 3, or 5. Therefore it is obvious that only by a definite assur-

ance that the tone of resolution is 1, 3 or 5, can we be sure that the tone in question is 2, 4 or 6.

For this reason it is good practice continually to review the groups which contain only 1, 3, 5 and 8. Make it a daily habit to sing 1 3 5 8, in order that you may become positive in your determination of 1, 3, 5 and 8. Thus you will solve the next question, because at the same time you will become positive of 7, 2, 4 and 6.

(2) *Exercises for Singing and Dictation:*
Study of the 6th Step.

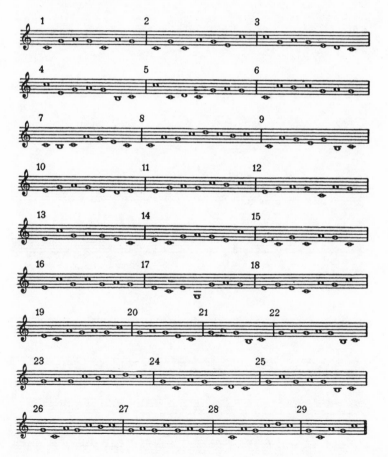

Study of 4th Step.

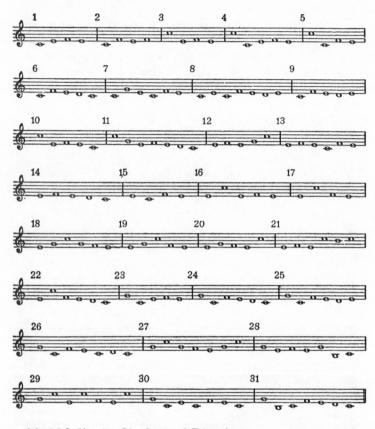

(3) *Melodies for Singing and Dictation:*

The above should be memorized and rewritten in different keys and time-values, as suggested before on page 38.

(4) *Exercises in Sight-Singing:*

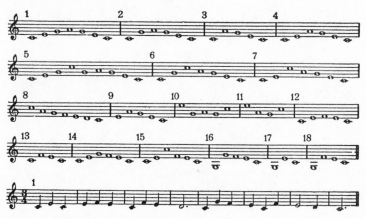

CHAPTER VII

The Minor Mode

The term *Mode* means style or manner. In music it applies to the arrangement of the whole and half-steps in the scale. We commonly use the *Major Mode* and the *Minor Mode;* major meaning greater; minor, lesser.

The *Minor Mode* is formed by lowering by one half-tone the third and sixth degrees of the Major. The general impression of the minor mode is that it is sad and gloomy, while the major is bright. This may be somewhat true, yet one of the most sad and impressive of funeral marches, the march from Handel's *Saul*, is in major. Many of our gay and popular tunes, like the Irish and Scotch dance-tunes, are in minor.

The *Minor Scale* is formed by lowering the third and sixth degrees of the major scale. This brings the half-steps between the second and third, fifth and sixth, seventh and eighth degrees. C major and c minor have the same letters for each degree; the pitch of the third degree (E in major) is changed to Eb in minor; of the sixth degree (A in major) is changed to Ab in minor. The first, second, fourth, fifth and seventh degrees remain the same.

Rest Tones (1 3 5 8) are the same in major and minor.

Active Tones (2 4 6 7) are the same in major and minor. They resolve in the same manner.

Capital letters are used for major, small letters for minor (C major, c minor).

Each major scale may be made minor by lowering the third and sixth degrees.

Major and minor scales with the same Tonic are *Parallel Major* and *Minor Scales*.

Lesson 8

Section A.

Suggestions for Study:
(1) Write the major scale from all pitches in treble and bass

[45]

with major signature. Make them minor by lowering one half-
tone the third and sixth steps. Example:

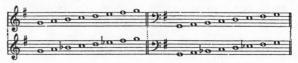

(2) Make the following major melodies minor.

(3) Complete the following, the second measure with an
added beat on accented pulse, the third measure with a divided
beat. (The first measure shows the meter and rhythmic unit.)
Review Chapter III for Added and Divided Beats.

Section B.

(1) Minor Mode:

(a) The minor scale of c is derived from the major scale of
C by lowering the 3rd and 6th steps.

Sing: 1 2 3 4 5 6 7 8 in C; sing it again, lowering
the 3rd and 6th. The result is c minor.

Sing: 8 7 6 5 4 3 2 1, first in C, then in c.

Practise the scale, first in major, then in minor, ascending and
descending from any pitch. The minor can be clearly understood
only by constantly comparing it with the major mode of the same
name. Thus, C major and c minor, and G major and g minor;
F major and f minor; etc.

(b) Sing 1 3 5 8 in C major; make it minor by lowering
the 3rd.

Sing 8 5 3 1 in the same way.

Play 1 3 1 $\overline{7}$ 1 in major; make it minor by lowering
the 3rd. Pause on 7. It will resolve as in major.

Play 1 3 1 2 in major and minor. 2 will resolve to 1 or 3 in minor as in major.

Play 1 3 4 3   1 4 3.

Play 1 3 5 6 5   1 6 5; 4 and 6 resolve the same.

C major and c minor are two expressions or modes of the *same* key. The difference between the modes is superficial; the likeness is fundamental.

(2) (a) Sing each of the following groups first in major and then in minor, lowering the 3rd and 6th. Sing each several times, changing from major to minor and from minor to major, until you realize the similarity of effect and at the same time the difference in the color or quality. As before, use the piano as a test of accuracy.

1 3 5 3 1	1 3 5 6 5 3 1	1 5 6 5 1 $\overline{7}$ 1	1 2 1 4 3 2 1
1 2 3 4 5 3 1	1 3 5 6 5	1 3 4 3 2 1	1 8 5 3 1 2 3
1 3 3 1	1 5 6 5	1 3 4 3 2 3 1	1 8 5 6 5 3 1
1 5 3 2 1	1 2 1 $\overline{7}$ 1	1 5 6 5 3 8	8 1 3 5 3 2 1
1 5 5 1	1 3 2 1 $\overline{7}$ 1	1 $\overline{7}$ 1 3 5 3 1	8 5 3 1 2 3 1

3 2 1 3 5 3 1	3 4 3 5 6 5	3 4 3 5 6 5 8 $\underline{2}$ 8
3 2 1 3 5 4 3	3 5 4 3 1 $\overline{7}$ 1	3 2 1 5 4 3 8 7 8
3 2 1 3 1	3 5 8 $\underline{2}$ 8	3 1 5 3 1 3 1
3 4 3 5 1	3 5 6 5 8 7 8	3 1 5 6 5 3 8

5 3 1 2 3 2 1	5 1 8 1 3 2 1	5 1 2 1 3 2 1
5 3 5 8 5 3 1	5 $\overline{7}$ 1 3 1	5 $\overline{7}$ 1 3 1 2 1
5 3 5 6 5 3 8	5 8 $\underline{2}$ 8 $\underline{3}$ 8	5 1 $\overline{7}$ 1 3 5 1
5 8 7 8 5 3 1	5 8 7 8 5 3 1	5 $\overline{7}$ 1 3 5 8

1 3 2 3 1 $\overline{7}$ 1	3 1 5 4 3 2 1	5 1 5 $\overline{5}$ 1 2 3
1 5 4 3 4 3 1	3 1 6 5 6 5 8	5 $\overline{5}$ 5 $\overline{7}$ 1 3 1
5 6 5 3 4 3 2 1	5 1 6 5 1 2 1	3 4 5 $\overline{7}$ 1 4 3
5 4 3 2 3 2 1	5 $\overline{7}$ 1 6 5 3 8	3 4 5 8 5 4 3
5 $\overline{7}$ 1 2 3 4 3	5 8 7 8 5 4 3	3 1 $\overline{7}$ 1 3 2 3
5 6 5 3 1 2 1	5 8 $\underline{2}$ 8 5 3 5	5 3 4 3 5 6 5
		8 7 8 5 6 5 1
		8 $\underline{2}$ 8 5 $\overline{7}$ 1 2 1

(b) After singing each of the above groups in major and in minor, sing through the entire series in minor.

(3) The following groups may be sung, and also used for dictation. Sing in minor and also in major, disregarding the accidentals.

Change the mode for each group several times. Then sing through the entire series in minor.

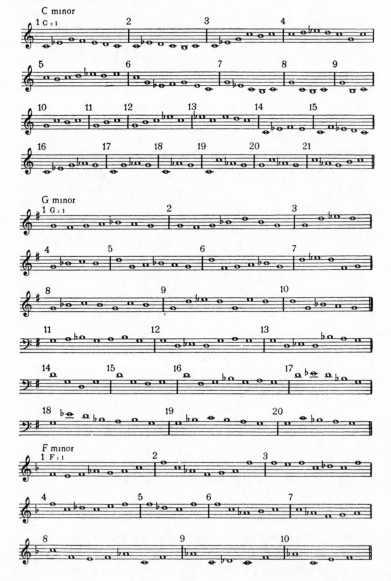

Section C.

Study of the Divided Beat:
(1) Tap 1 2 and intone the following:

Then divide the beat, tapping 1 2:

The meter or regular pulsation is always physical and may be represented by movement of the arm or foot. All rhythms, i. e., subdivisions, are mental and should be thought, not indicated by physical movement.

Learn the arm-movements down–up ↓₁ ↑² to indicate the beat. Repeat the above, using the arm-movements instead of tapping.

Practise the following:

(2) *For Practice in Singing and Dictation:*
Rhythm and Pitch in minor.

After writing, rewrite in a different note-value.

(3) *Exercises in Sight-Singing:*
   (a) Sing each exercise in Major, using numbers and letters.
   (b) Repeat, making it minor by lowering the 3rd and 6th
       steps.

CHAPTER VIII

Minor Signatures

Minor Keys have no signatures of their own.

Composers, when seeking variety, often repeat a few measures of a major melody, keeping the same tones and major signature, but make it minor by lowering the third and sixth steps. For example:

Beethoven

1 Phrase in major   2 Repetition of Phrase 1 made minor by lowering C

Composers, when writing an entire composition in minor, *borrow* a major signature, which lowers the third and sixth steps of the major key. This saves the labor of writing accidentals before these tones. The signature for the minor key is borrowed from the major key of the same name as the third step of the minor scale.

As the borrowed signature lowers not only the third and sixth steps but also the seventh step of the major, it will always be necessary to raise the seventh step.

Major and minor keys with the same signature are called *Relative* Major and Minor keys.

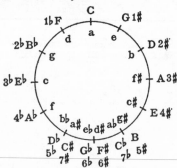

NOTE: C minor and E♭ major are not the same keys. They are different tonalities, having different rest and active tones. C major and c minor are the same tonalities, having the same rest and active tones. Only the mode is changed.

As the major keys were arranged on the clock, the minor keys may be placed opposite the major keys with the same signatures. The keys of a♭, d♯ and a♯ minor are seldom used. G♯ minor, the relative of B major, has no parallel major key.

[52]

Section A.

Suggestions for Study:

(1) Write, in the treble and bass, the major scale from all pitches with the major signatures. Make them minor by lowering the third and sixth steps. Under each write the same minor scale with the borrowed signature. Raise the seventh step.

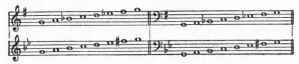

(2) Place the following scale-steps in treble and bass in keys of a, e, b and f♯ minor, using borrowed signatures: 1 3 5 6 5 7 8.

(3) Place the following scale-steps in treble and bass in keys of c♯, g♯, d and g minor, using borrowed signatures: 8 5 6 5 4 3 2 5 1.

(4) Place the following scale-steps in treble and bass in keys of f, b♭ and e♭ minor, using borrowed signatures: 1 5 3 6 5 7 8.

Section B.

(1) *Exercises for pitch.* To be used for singing and dictation.

(a) Sing by numbers.

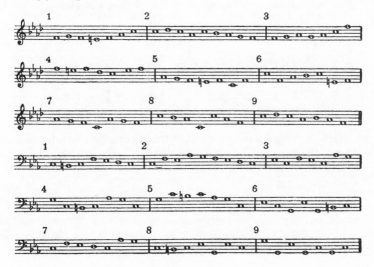

(2) *Exercises for Dictation and Memorizing:*

(a) After writing in major, alter to minor with accidentals and sing in minor by numbers.

(b) Write from memory in minor with proper signatures.

NOTE. In dictating melodies with divided beats, first play the melody through with a simple accompaniment to establish the pulsation and tempo. For example, Nos. 1 and 3 could be played this way:

After the pupil has determined the meter, he should make an outline of the four measures, using dots to represent the pulses.

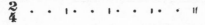

As the melody is replayed, place the pencil on a dot at each recurrence of the pulse. Decide how many notes there are to the pulse, or if there is one note for two pulses. When there is one note to the pulse, leave the dot. If there are two notes, write 2

under the dot. **If one** note for two pulses, tie the dots. The rhythm
of No. 1 would be outlined $\frac{2}{4}$ • • | • • | • • | ‿• ‖

After the rhythmic **outline is** made, write the numbers of the
pitches in the usual way.

(3) *Exercises in Sight-Singing:*

Section C.

(1) The Divided Beat in 3/4.

Tap 1 2 3 and intone the following:

Dividing the beat:

$$\begin{array}{ccc} \text{♫♪♫} & \text{♫♪♫♪♫} & \text{♫♪♫♫} & \text{♩.} \\ 1 \quad 2 \quad 3 & 1 \quad 2 \quad 3 & 1 \quad 2 \quad 3 & 1 \ 2 \ 3 \end{array}$$

Arm-movements for 3/4 are Down–right–up

Practise the following:

(a)   ♩ ♩ ♩   ♫♪♫   ♩ ♩ ♩   ♩.
       1   2   3   1   2   3   etc.
       Down right up,   down right up,   etc.

(b) ...

(c) ...

(d) ...

(e) ...

(f) ...

(g) ...

(h) ...

(i) ...

(j) ...

(k) ...

(2) *Exercises for Dictation, Memorizing and Singing:*
     (a) After writing in major, alter to minor with accidentals.
     (b) Write from memory with customary minor signatures.

(3) *Exercises in Sight-Singing:*

Section A.

Suggestions for Study:

(1) Write the following scale-steps in treble, first in A major, then in a minor, lowering 3rd and 6th steps of major; then in a

minor, using borrowed signature: 1 8 6 5 3 4 2 5 3 5 7̄ 1.

(2) Write the following scale-steps as above, in the bass, first in C major, then in c minor: 8 7 8 3 5 4 3 2 6 5 7 8 3 2 1.

(3) Write as above in the treble in E major, then in e minor: 8 5 7 8 6 4 2 3 1 6 5 7 8.

(4) Write as above in the bass in B major and b minor: 1 6 5 7 8 3 4 2 3 5 1.

(5) Write as above in the treble in F major and f minor: 1 4 2 5 3 6 4 2 7̄ 1.

(6) Learn to recite the borrowed signature of each minor key.

(7) Learn the seventh step of each minor key.

Section B.

(1) All active tones may defer their resolution by a skip of a third in the direction of their normal resolution.

Thus, 7 may resolve 7 2 1, instead of going directly to 1.

Sing 1 7̄ 1   3 1 7̄ 2 1   5 3 1 7̄ 2 1
      1 2 1   3 5 1 7̄ 2 1   5 8 3 1 7̄ 2 1
      1 7̄ 1 2 1   3 1 5̄ 1 7̄ 2 1   5 5̄ 1 7̄ 2 1
      1 7̄ 2 1   5 8 3 5 1 7̄ 2 1

(2) Thus, 2 may resolve 2 7 1, instead of 2 1.

Sing 1 3 2 1   3 1 2 7̄ 1   5 3 1 2 7̄ 1   1 2 7̄ 1 3 5
      1 2 7̄ 1   3 5 1 2 7̄ 1   5 3 2 7̄ 1   1 2 7̄ 1 5 1
      1 3 2 7̄ 1   3 5̄ 1 2 7̄ 1   5 5̄ 1 2 7̄ 1   3 2 7̄ 1 3 1
      1 5 3 2 7̄ 1   3 5 5̄ 1 2 7̄ 1   5 8 1 2 7̄ 1   3 2 7̄ 1 5̄ 1 3
      1 2 7̄ 1 3 5 8   3 1 5̄ 1 2 7̄ 1   5 8 3 2 7̄ 1

(3) Repeat the above in minor.

(4) *Exercises for Singing and Dictation* in major; then in minor.

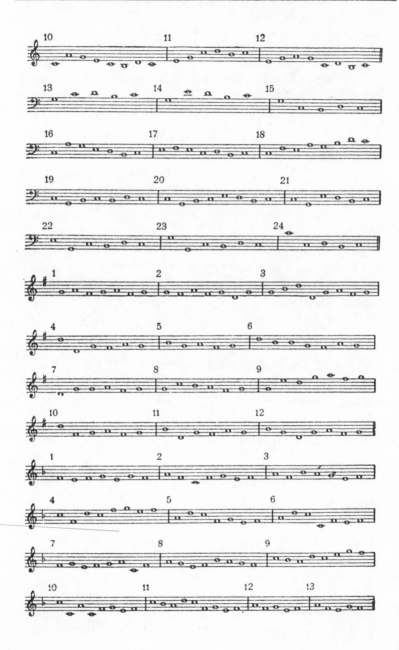

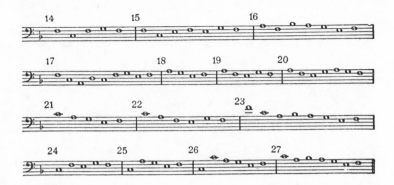

Section C.

(1) *Exercises for Dictation in Major:*
  (a) After writing, sing in minor.
  (b) Write from memory in minor, using minor signature.

(2) *Exercises in Sight-Singing:*

CHAPTER IX

Intervals

The difference in the pitch of two tones is an *Interval*. Intervals are measured along the major scale from the lower tone as Tonic. They are placed in the major scale of the lower tone and named from the number of degrees or steps the tones are distant from each other. If the upper tone is the 5th step of the scale of the lower tone, the interval is a fifth; if the 4th step, a fourth; etc.

Intervals are measured to the octave inclusive. Beyond the octave a new series is begun. Occasionally ninths and tenths are used, but these are treated like seconds and thirds.

P. Prime   M 2   M 3   P 4   P 5   M 6   M 7   P 8   M 9   M 10

Lesson 11

Major and Perfect Intervals

The intervals formed in a major scale, taking its tonic as the lower tone, are primes, seconds, thirds, fourths, fifths, sixths, sevenths and octaves. There are two titles given to these intervals. The primes, fourths, fifths and octaves are called *Perfect Intervals*, because the tones forming these intervals are the most nearly related in their number of vibrations. The seconds, thirds, sixths and sevenths are called *Major Intervals*. In speaking of an interval, the title is always used. A fifth is a Perfect Fifth, a second a Major Second, just as John Smith, a doctor, is Doctor Smith, or Frank Jones, a major, is Major Jones.

Section A.

Suggestions for Study:

(1) Learn to recite the intervals from the tonic of a major scale. Thus: 1 to 1, a perfect prime; 1 to 2, a major 2nd; 1 to 3, a major 3rd; 1 to 4, a perfect 4th; etc.

(2) Write the perfect intervals from the tonic of the scales of G, F, D, B♭ and A major (using signatures).

Write the major intervals from the tonic of the scales of E♭, E, A♭, B, D♭ major (using signatures).

[64]

(3) Write the perfect intervals, using accidentals, from the

notes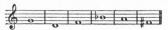

Write the major interval, using accidentals, from the notes

Section B.

The Major Third.

(1) Play this: striking the tones together. This is known as an Harmonic Interval.

Sing the lower tone, calling it 1, and then the higher tone, calling it 3. Name the interval. Listen carefully to this sound. You have learned to recognize 1 and 3 played separately. Now practise recognizing them played together as an interval.

(2) Play the tone G; call it 1. Sing 1 3. Play the tones G and B together as an harmonic interval:

(3) Play F; call it 1. Sing 1 3.
Play F–A as an harmonic interval.
Play D; call it 1. Sing 1 3.
Play D–F♯ as an harmonic interval.
Play B♭. Call it 1. Sing 1 3.
Play B♭–D as an harmonic interval.

(4) Play the following:

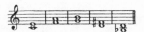

After playing each, sing the lower tone 1 and then the higher tone. Afterward, sing 3 first and then 1.

(5) *Pitch Drill:*

(a) 2 may also resolve 2 4 3, instead of 2 3.

Sing in major and minor, using numbers and letters, in the keys of C, F and G.

1 2 3	3 1 2 4 3	5 3 2 4 3	8 5 3 2 4 3
1 2 4 3	3 2 4 3 1	5 3 2 4 3 5 8	8 1 2 4 3
1 2 4 3 2 1	3 2 4 3 5	5 3 2 4 3 2 1	8 2̲ 8 1 2 4 3
1 7̄ 1 3 2 4 3	3 2 4 3 1 7̄ 1		
1 3 2 4 3 2 1	3 1 7̄ 1̣ 2 4 3		
1 5 1 2 3 2 4 3			
1 8 1 7̄ 1 2 4 3			

(b) Write on the staff in the keys of C, F and G major
    and minor.

(6) 4 may resolve 4 2 3, instead of 4 3.

Sing 1 3 4 3
     1 3 4 2 3

Or 4 may resolve 4 2 1.

Sing 1 3 4 2 1.   Sing 1 3 4 2 3.   Sing 1 3 4 2 1.

(a) Sing in major and minor, using numbers and letters, in
the keys of C, F and G.

1 3 2 4 3 4 2 1	1 2 1 4 2 1	3 1 2 3 4 2 1	5 3 4 2 1 7̄ 1
1 3 5 4 2 1	1 2 1 4 2 3	3 1 2 3 4 2 3	5 1 4 3 4 2 1
1 3 4 2 1 7̄ 1	1 3 1 4 2 3	3 1 4 3 4 2 1	5 8 3 5 4 2 1
1 3 4 2 3 5 8	1 3 1 4 2 1	3 1 4 3 4 2 3	5 1 4 2 3 2 1
1 4 3 4 2 1		3 5 1 3 4 2 1	8 5 3 4 2 1
1 7̄ 1 4 3 4 2 3		3 5 5̄ 1 4 2 3	8 3 5 4 2 3
			8 3 5 4 2 3 2 1

(b) Write on the staff in the keys of C, F and G major
and minor.

(7) *Exercises in Sight-Singing:*

Section C.

The Perfect Fifth:

(1) Play this:

Sing the lower tone (1) and then the higher (5). Play it again as an harmonic interval. Name it.

Play this: Play the 5th, then the 3rd, several times, comparing the two sounds. Note the empty, hollow sound of the 5th as contrasted with the full, round sound of the 3rd.

Sing 1 5. Sing 1 3 5. Note that the 3rd fills in the hollowness of the 5th.

Sing a perfect 5th up from the following tones. First play each tone, taking it as 1:

NOTE. A 5th may always be found by first thinking 1 3 5.

After singing each 5th, play it as an harmonic interval.
Play the following:

Sing the tones 1 and then 5.   Afterwards sing 5 and then 1.

(2) *Exercises for Dictation:*

Melodies containing 2 4 3 and 4 2 3.   Each may be written in other keys and time-values, and used for singing.

(3) *Exercises in Sight-Singing:*

LESSON 12

Minor Intervals

The title of the Interval determines its *Quality*. The quality of an interval may be changed by altering the pitch of either tone one half or one whole step. This alteration of the pitch of either tone of the interval does not change the number-name of the interval. E to B is always a 5th, even if the pitch of B is changed to Bb, or E to E♯.

The Perfect and Major Intervals, formed from the tonic to the other steps of the major scale, are used as a standard of measurement.

If a Major Interval is made one half-tone smaller, its title is changed to *Minor*. Therefore, there are major and minor 2nds, 3rds, 6ths and 7ths.

> NOTE. The terms *major* and *minor*, as applied to intervals, have no connection with the same terms as applied to scales, except as they mean *greater* or *lesser*.

Section A.

Suggestions for Study:

(1) Write the Minor Intervals from the tonic of the keys of A, G, B♭, F♯, E♭ and B major.

(2) Write the Minor Intervals, using accidentals, from the

notes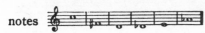

Section B.

(1) The Perfect Fourth (5 8) and Minor Sixth (3 8).

    (a) Play 1 3 5 8 from C.

        Think 1 3 5 5 8. Think 5 8. Sing it. Test on piano.

        Write it on staff thus:

        Play it as an harmonic interval. Name it.

        Play 1 3 5 8 from G, F, D and B♭, and study the perfect fourth as outlined as above.

        Play the following:

        Sing the lower tone, calling it 5, and the upper tone, calling it 8. Afterwards play each interval, and sing 8 first and then 5. The perfect fourth from 5 to 8 is one of the most commonly used intervals. A great many songs begin with it.

    (b) Play 1 3 5 8 from C.

        Think 1 3 3 5 8. Sing 3 5 8. Sing 3 8. Test on piano

> Write 3 8 on staff. Name it. Play it as an harmonic
> interval. Sing it again after playing, singing 3 and
> then 8. Play again, and sing 8 and then 3.
> Play 1 3 5 8 from G, F, D and B♭.
> Practise the minor 6th in each key as outlined above.
> Play the following:

(2) *Pitch Drill:*

6 may resolve 6 4 3 instead of 6 5.

Sing:—

1 3 5 6 5	3 5 6 5	5 6 5 3 1	5 8 5 6 4 3	8 2̲ 7 8 5 6 4 3
1 3 5 6 4 3 2 1	3 5 6 4 3	5 6 4 3 2 1	8 5 6 4 3 2 1	1 2̅ 7 1 6 4 3
1 3 5 6 4 3	3 1 6 5 3	5 1 6 5 3	8 3 5 6 4 3	5̅ 7̅ 1 6 4 3
1 6 5 3 1	3 1 6 4 3	5 1 6 4 3 2 1	8 1 6 5 3	5̅ 7̅ 2 1 6 4 3
1 6 4 3 1	3 5 1 6 5 3	5 1 6 4 3	8 1 6 4 3	
1 6 4 3 2 1	3 5 1 6 4 3	5 6 4 3		

The above numbers should be written on the staff in C, F and
G, treble and bass. Then they should be referred to later and
sung from the staff by number and letter. They should also be
used for dictation. After they have become comparatively easy
in major, they should be studied in minor by lowering the 3rd and
6th. They should also be written in c, f and g minor and sung
by number.

(3) *Exercises for Dictation:*

Melodies containing 6 4, for dictation and singing:

These should be written in other keys and in the minor mode, and with different note-values.

Section C.

Pitch Drill:

(1) The skip 4 6 5 is also used.

Sing 1 3 5 6 5   5 3 4 6 5 7̄ 1
      1 3 4 6 5 3 1   8 5 3 4 6 5
      1 3 4 6 5 3 8   8 3 4 6 5
      3 5 4 6 5   8 1 4 6 5
      5 3 4 6 5   8 2̲ 8 3 4 6 5
      5 3 4 6 5 3 8

The above numbers to be written as directed in **Lesson 12,** Section B, page 71.

(2) *Exercises for Dictation and Singing:*

Melodies containing any of the skips 7 2, 2 4, 6 4, 4 6.

The above should be written in other keys; also in minor and with different note-values.

(3) *Exercises in Sight-Singing:*

LESSON 13

The Up-beat

Rhythm in music may begin with the accented or the unaccented pulse of the meter. This corresponds to the rhythm or kind of foot used in poetry. If the rhythm begins with the accented pulse, the effect is — ⌣ or a trochee. If the rhythm begins with the unaccented pulse the effect is ⌣ — or an iambus.

When the rhythm begins on the accented pulse, the measure will correspond to the space between the bars, thus:

1. Ma - ry, ·Ma - ry, quite con - tra - ry

When the rhythm begins on the unaccented pulse in duple meter, a measure will extend from the unaccented through the accented pulse, thus:

2. The shades of   night were fall - ing fast

When the rhythm begins on the unaccented pulse in triple meter, a measure will extend from the second unaccented through the first unaccented pulse, thus:

3. A - long came a   spi - der and   sat down be - side her

Section A.

Suggestions for Study:

(1) Erect (using accidentals) a Perfect 5th ⎫
                             Minor 6th ⎪
                             Major 2nd ⎬ from
                             Perfect 4th ⎪ E, A, D, G, B
                             Minor 3rd ⎪ and F♯.
                             Major 7th ⎭

(2) Erect (using accidentals) a Major 3rd
Minor 2nd
Major 6th } from
Perfect 5th Db Ab, C, F,
Minor 7th Bb and Eb.

(3) Name the following intervals:

(4) Scan the following lines, marking the long and short syllables:

Jack and Jill went up the hill.
Rock-a-by baby on the tree-top.
Sing a song o' sixpence.
Humpty Dumpty sat on the wall.
Maxwelton's braes are bonny.
Flow gently, sweet Afton.
O say, can you see, by the dawn's early light.
By yon bonnie banks and by yon bonnie braes.

(5) Make rhythmic outlines of each, as in Examples **1, 2** and **3**, page 74.

Section B.

(1) (a) Play the following:

Sing each; first the lower tone (3), and then the higher (8).
Play each again, and sing 8 first and then **3**.
(b) Play 1 3 5 8 from C.
Think 1 5. Think 5 8.

Play the following:

Sing each, singing the lower tone first. Note the
resemblance in quality between the fifth and
fourth; but the difference in the quantity of each
interval due to its position in the scale.

Repeat this practice in the keys of G, F, D and B♭.

(c) Play 1 3 5 8 from C.
     Think 1 3. Think 3 8.

     Play the following: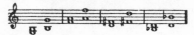

Sing each, singing the lower tone first. Note the resemblance in quality and difference in quantity.

Repeat this practice in the keys of G, F, D and B♭.

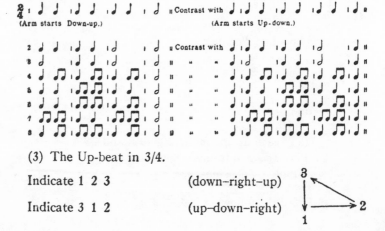

(2) The Up-beat in 2/4.

Practise these exercises as follows:

Intone the rhythm.

Use the arm to indicate the beat. Down–up, down–up—

↓₁ ↑² indicates 1–2, 1–2. Up-down, up–down indicates 2–1, 2–1.

(3) The Up-beat in 3/4.

Indicate 1 2 3   (down–right–up)

Indicate 3 1 2   (up–down–right)

Intone the rhythm and beat the meter.

(4) The Key of D.

    (a) In beginning the study of a new key turn to any of the groups of numbers in the preceding pages and practise singing them, using the letter-names of the new key. After singing a group, write it on the staff in both clefs.

    (b) For practice of the new skips 8 6 5, 8 4 3, 8 2 1, Play d¹. Think 1 3 5 8.

Sing		
8 5 6 5	8 5 3 4 3	8 1 2 1
8 6 5	8 3 4 3	8 2 1
8 6 5 3 1	8 4 3	8 2 3 2 1
8 6 5 7̄ 1	8 4 3 5 8	8 2 1 7̄ 1
8 6 5 3 5	8 1 8 4 3	1 8 2 1
1 8 6 5	8 1 8 6 5	3 8 2 1
3 8 6 5	8 6 5 8 4 3	5 8 2 1
5 8 6 5	3 8 4 3	5 1 8 2 1
3 5 8 6 5	3 5 8 4 3	3 1 8 2 1
5 3 8 6 5	3 1 8 4 3	3 5 8 2 1
5 7̄ 1 8 6 5	5 3 8 4 3	5 3 8 2 1
8 2̲ 8 6 5	5 1 8 4 3	8 2̲ 8 2 1
8 3̲ 8 6 5	8 2̲ 8 4 3	8 3̲ 8 2 1
8 6 5 7 8	8 3̲ 8 4 3	8 2 1 7̄ 1
	8 4 3 2 1	8 2 1 5̄ 1

(5) The following groups are to be practised:

    (a) Recite the numbers of a group.
    (b) Play 1 3 5 8 from D.
    (c) Think the sound of the group.
    (d) Sing the group, with numbers and letters, and test on piano.

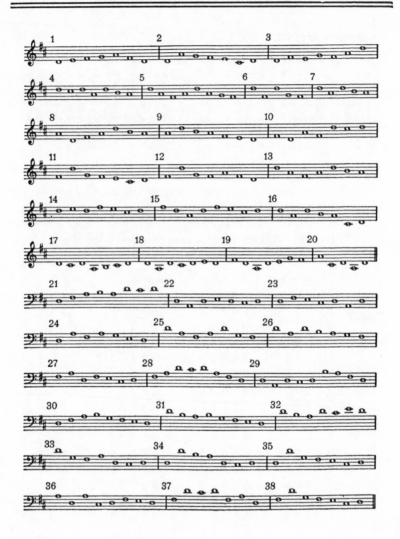

Section C.

(1) Play the following tones: C, F, G, D, Bb. Call each tone 1 and sing the major 3rd and perfect 5th up from it. Play the 3rd and 5th harmonically after singing them. Try to determine for yourself the different quality in the sound of the 3rd and the 5th.

(2) *Phrases for Dictation:*

   (a) Have one of the melodies beginning on the down-beat dictated.

   (b) Decide meter.

   (c) Represent the pulses and outline the rhythm.

   (d) Write the numbers.

   (e) Place on the staff.

   (f) After the melody (a) has been played, the melody (a^1) should be played. Contrast the two, and then write (a^1) on the staff.

NOTE. The up-beat is easily felt and recognized when it is associated with breathing; the accented pulse being felt as the exhalation, breathing; the un-accented pulse as the inhalation.

(3) *Exercises in Sight-Singing:*

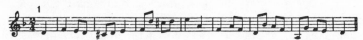

LESSON 14

Diminished and Augmented Intervals

If a Perfect Interval or a Minor Interval is made one half-tone smaller, it becomes a *Diminished Interval*. There are diminished primes, 2nds, 3rds, 4ths, 5ths, 6ths, 7ths and octaves.

If a Perfect Interval or a Major Interval is made one half-tone larger, it becomes an *Augmented Interval*. There are augmented primes, 2nds, 3rds, 4ths, 5ths, 6ths, 7ths and octaves.

To name an interval, regard the lower tone as the Tonic of a major scale. The number of degrees from the lower tone to the higher gives the size of the interval. If the upper tone agrees with the major scale of the lower tone, the interval will be either major or perfect. If it is one half-tone smaller than a major interval, it is called minor; if one half-tone smaller than the perfect or minor interval, it is diminished; if one half-tone larger than the perfect or major interval, it is augmented.

Compound Meter

Duple, triple and quadruple meters are known as simple meters. All rhythms used in 2/4, 3/4 and 4/4 are made by adding the pulses or dividing a quarter-note by two or a multiple of two with the exceptional subdivision into three or five. If a constant triplet subdivision is desired, the *Compound Meters* are used.

A six-pulse meter is a duple meter, each pulse divided into triplets:

List of Rhythms:

A nine-pulse meter is a triple meter, each pulse divided into triplets: All rhythms used in 6/8 will recur in 9/8.

A twelve-pulse meter is a quadruple meter, each pulse divided into triplets: All rhythms used in 6/8 will recur in 12/8.

Section A.

Suggestions for Study:

(1) Erect (using accidentals) an
> Augmented 8th
> Diminished 5th
> Minor 3rd
> Diminished 4th } from D, A, F, C and E.
> Augmented 6th
> Augmented 4th
> Minor 7th

(2) Erect (using accidentals) a
> Diminished 8th
> Minor 2nd
> Diminished 3rd
> Perfect 4th } from C, A, E, C♯ and F♯.
> Augmented 5th
> Minor 6th
> Diminished 7th

NOTE. In the exercises given above the augmented and diminished intervals are to be written using the given tone as lower tone. If a given interval is to be made augmented or diminished, it is generally made augmented by raising the higher tone; made diminished by raising the lower tone.

The terms raise and lower are used instead of sharp and flat, as a natural is also used to raise or lower the pitch of tones.

If the higher tone of an interval is raised the interval is larger. If the lower tone is raised the interval is smaller.

```
················Higher tone            ————————Higher tone
————————Lower tone                     ················Lower tone
```

If the higher tone is lowered, the interval becomes smaller. If the lower tone is lowered, the interval is larger.

```
················Higher tone            ————————Higher tone
————————Lower tone                     ················Lower tone
```

(3) Name the following intervals:

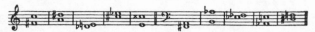

(4) Write examples four measures in length, of 4/4 and 6/8 meters, using added and divided beats. The rhythms may be copied from a composition.

Section B.

(1) (a) Play the following:

(b) Sing each, singing the lower tone first—using the number and letter-names. If played in a register impossible for singing, think the separate sounds.

(c) Name the interval.

(2) Study of 4/4 Meter:

Tap the beat 1–2–3–4, and intone the rhythm.

Use your arm to indicate the beat: down, left, right, up.

(3) *Phrases for Dictation:*

(a) Represent the rhythm.

(b) Write numbers.

(c) Place on the staff.

Section C.

(1) Study of 4/4 Meter, added beat:

Tap the beat or use the arm-movement—down, left, right, up. Intone the rhythm:

(2) *Phrases for Dictation and Sight-Singing:*

(a) Decide the meter.
(b) Decide up-beat or down-beat.
(c) Represent the rhythm.
(d) Write the numbers.
(e) Represent on the staff.

LESSON 15

Section A.

Suggestions for Study:

(1) Erect, using accidentals, an Augmented 2nd
                                a Major 6th
                            an Augmented 5th   } from G,
                            a Diminished 7th   B,A,Bb,
                            a Minor 6th   Gb.
                            a Perfect 4th

(2) Erect, using accidentals, a Minor 3rd
                                an Augmented 4th
                            a Diminished 7th   } from Cb,
                            a Perfect 5th   B, G, A,
                            a Diminished 2nd   Eb.
                            a Major 7th

(3) Name the following intervals:

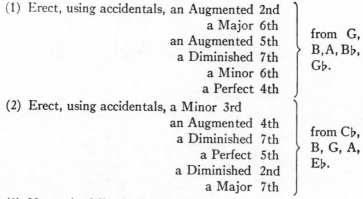

(4) Write examples, four measures in length, of 4/4 and 6/8 meters, using an added beat and a divided beat.

Section B.

(1) The Minor Third (3–5).

    (a) Play 1 3 5 8 from C.

        Think 1 3 3 5.   Think 3 5.   Sing.   Test.

        Think 1.   Sing 3 5.   Write on staff.

        Name the interval.

        Play 1 3 5 8 from G, F, D and B♭, and study the minor 3rd in each key as outlined above.

    (b) Play the following:

        Sing each; the lower tone first, calling it 3; then the higher tone, calling it 5.   Each of these minor 3rds is 3 to 5 in a major key.

    (c) Play each.   Think the tones as 3 5.   Sing 1.   If this is, at first, difficult you may play 1, but try to think it, and practise constantly until you can do it easily.

    (d) Play the following notes: E, A, B, F♯, D.   Call each in turn 3.   Think 3 1.   Place on the staff.   Name.   Think 3 5.   Place on the staff and name.

    (e) In each of the following groups play the open note, think and sing the black note.

(2) 4/4 meter, divided beat.

In the following exercises intone the rhythm and tap the beat.

(3) *Melodies for Dictation and Singing:*

Section C.

(1) The Major Sixth (5 <u>3</u>).
   (a) Play 1 3 5 8 from C.
      Think 5 8; 5 8 <u>3</u>; 5 <u>3</u>. Sing 5 <u>3</u>. Test.
     Place on staff.   Name the interval.

Play 1 3 5 8 from F, G, D and B♭, and study the major
6th in each key as outlined above.

(b) Play the following:

Sing each; the lower tone first, calling it 5; then the
higher tone, calling it <u>3</u>.

(c) If each 6th is 5 to upper 3, decide the key of each.
Play again. Sing the keynote (8) of each 6th.

(d) Play the following notes: G, C, D, A, F. Call each
in turn 5. Think 5 <u>3</u>. Place on the staff and name.

(2) *Exercises in Sight-Singing:*

LESSON 16

The Inversion of Intervals

Intervals are *inverted* by placing the lower tone one octave higher.

The interval C to E is a major 3rd, as E is the 3rd step of the scale of C. The inversion of C to E is E to C. The interval from E to C is a minor 6th, for C♯ (not C) is the 6th step of E. In the same manner the major 2nd, C to D, inverts to a minor 7th, D to C.

The perfect 4th, C to F, inverts to a perfect 5th, F to C. The perfect 5th, C to G, inverts to a perfect 4th, G to C. The major 6th, C to A, inverts to a minor 3rd, A to C. The major 7th, C to B, inverts to a minor 2nd, B to C. The minor 3rd, C to E♭, inverts to a major 6th, E♭ to C.

Maj. 3   Min. 6   Maj. 2   Min. 7   P. 4   P. 5   P. 5   P. 4   Maj. 6   Min. 3   Maj. 7   Min. 2   Min. 3   Maj. 6

The augmented 2nd, from C to D♯, inverts to a diminished 7th, D♯ to C. The diminished 5th, B to F, inverts to the augmented 4th, F to B.

Aug. 2   Dim. 7   Dim. 5   Aug. 4

From the above may be made the following table:
Upon inversion, a Major Interval becomes Minor.

"   "   a Perfect Interval remains Perfect.

"   "   an Augmented Interval becomes Diminished.

"   "   a 2nd becomes a 7th.

"   "   a 3rd becomes a 6th.

"   "   a 4th becomes a 5th.

NOTE. Both of these tables read from either side. A major 2nd becomes a minor 7th; a minor 7th becomes a major 2nd, etc.

Inversion of intervals saves time in naming intervals. For example, if the interval C down to E be named, it is much easier to think of it as a minor 6th, the inversion of the major 3rd C to E, than to think in the key of E, etc.

The intervals down from 8 are the inversions of the intervals up from 1. The intervals up from 1 are major and perfect. Down from 8, minor and perfect; 8 to 2, a 7th; 8 to 3, a 6th; etc.

Section A.

> *Suggestions for Study:*
> (1) Learn the table of *Inversions*.
> (2) Invert and name the following:

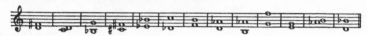

Section B.

> *For practice of the skips 5 2, 2 5.*
> (1) Play B♭.   Think 1 3 5 8.

Sing   8 5 8 2̲ 8   8 2̲ 5 8
         8 5 2̲ 8   3̲ 2̲ 5 8
         8 6 5 2̲ 8   1 2 5 1
         1 5 3 2 1   3 2 5 1
         1 5 2 1   5 3 1 2 5 **1**
         5 1 2 1   5 1 2 5 1
         5 2 1   5 3 2 5 1
         1 5 2 5 1   5 6 5 8 2̲ 5 8
         8 5 2̲ 5 8   5 6 5 1 2 5 1
         3 5 2 5 1   8 5 3 5 5 2 3
         3̲ 5 2̲ 5 8   3 2 5 4 3 5 8
                           1 3 5 6 5 2 3

(2) 4/4 meter.   Up-beat.   Arm-movement

Tap the beat and intone the rhythm.

(3) *Exercises for Practice in Dictation:*

Section C.

(1) Lesson 14 completed the study of the intervals which are found in combinations of 1 3 5 and 8, with the exception of the unison 1 to 1, and the perfect octave 1 to 8.

Following is a table showing the relation of these intervals when inverted.

1 – 1 Perfect prime (L 1)		1 – 8 Perfect octave (L 8)
1 – 3 Major 3rd (+3)	when	3 – 8 Minor 6th (−6)
1 – 5 Perfect 5th (L 5)	Inverted	5 – 8 Perfect 4th (L 4)
3 – 5 Minor 3rd (−3)	becomes	5 – 3 Major 6th (+6)

Success in studying intervals depends upon the ability to construct any combination of 1 3 5 8 from any tone.   Practice along this line is helpful beyond all calculation, since it not only gives a positive knowledge of useful intervals, but also a method of thinking which develops the ability in melodic dictation and sight-singing.

Below are three arrangements of all the intervals in the keys thus far studied.

In (A) the intervals are arranged by inversion.

In (B) all intervals having the same lower tone are grouped together.

In (C) there is no plan of arrangement, these being only for practice after A and B have been thoroughly studied and practised.

These lists are for practice and constant reference. Each student should have (A) and (B) clearly in mind and write out such arrangements from memory.

As a new key is studied, arrange and study the intervals in this manner.

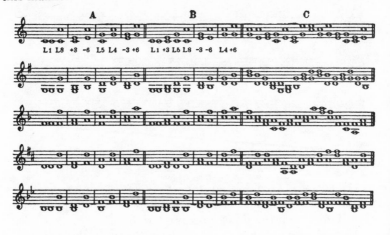

(2) *Exercises in Sight-Singing:*

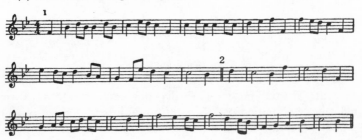

Lesson 17

Staff and Scale Position of Intervals

The position on the staff and in the major scale of the most used intervals should be learned. This saves the trouble of measuring the intervals. Following is a table of intervals on the staff and in the major scale.

Staff:

    Maj. 2nds.   All but E–F, B–C, which are minor.
    Maj. 3rds.   C–E, F–A, and G–B. Others minor.
    Per. 4ths.   All except F–B, which is augmented.
    Per. 5ths.   All except B–F, which is diminished.
    Maj. 6ths.   C–A, D–B, F–D, and G–E. Others minor.
    Maj. 7ths.   C–B, F–E. Others minor.

Major Scale:

    Maj. 2nds.   All but 3–4, 7–8, which are minor.
    Maj. 3rds.   1–3, 4–6, 5–7. Others minor.
    Per. 4ths.   All but 4–7, which is augmented.
    Per. 5ths.   All but 7–4, which is diminished.
    Maj. 6ths.   1–6, 2–7, 4–2, 5–3. Others minor.
    Maj. 7ths.   1–7, 4–3. Others minor.

	Staff	Scale
Aug. 4ths.	F–B	4–7
Dim. 5ths.	B–F	7–4

Note. These are the only augmented and diminished intervals which occur on the staff or in the major scale without altering the pitch of tones with accidentals.

In a minor key the following *augmented* and *diminished intervals* occur, formed by the lowered 3rd and 6th steps:

Aug. 4th : 4–7; 6–2.   Aug. 2nd : 6–7.   Aug. 5th : 3–7.
Dim. 5th : 7–4; 2–6.   Dim. 7th : 7–6.   Dim. 4th : 7–3.

Intervals are *Consonant* when they sound finished and do not need resolution. Such intervals, found between the rest tones, are all the perfect intervals and the major and minor thirds and sixths.

Intervals are *Dissonant* when they require resolution. These are the major and minor 2nds and 7ths and all augmented and diminished intervals.

Section A.

Suggestions for Study:

(1) Learn the position on the staff of the *major* and *perfect intervals.*

(2) Learn the position in the major scale of the *major* and *perfect intervals.*

(3) Learn the position on the staff of the *augmented* and *diminished intervals.*

(4) Learn the position in the major scale of the *augmented* and *diminished intervals.*

(5) Learn the position in the minor scale of the *augmented* and *diminished intervals.*

(6) Write and resolve the augmented 4th and diminished 5th in keys of C, F, G, B and D major.

Write and resolve the augmented 2nd and diminished 7th in keys of c, a, g and b minor.

Write and resolve the two augmented 4ths and the diminished 5ths in keys of e, d, f and f♯ minor.

Write and resolve the augmented 5th, and diminished 4th, in keys of a, c, d and g minor.

Example: The augmented 4th and diminished 5th in a major scale are from 4–7 and 7–4.

Following are these intervals in the key of G major:

Aug. 4   Dim. 5

Following are the augmented intervals in g minor:

The tones of the intervals resolve according to the law of active and rest tones.

Section B.

(1) Practise the Intervals of Lesson 16, Section C, Page 92.

(2) *Exercises for Practice of the Skip* $\bar{5}$ 4, 4 $\bar{5}$:

Play a¹ as 1.   Think 1 3 5 8; 1 $\bar{5}$ 1 3 1.

Sing the following.

Write on the staff in keys of A major and a minor.

1 $\bar{5}$ 1 3 1	1 $\bar{6}$ $\bar{5}$ 4 3 1	1 3 1 $\bar{5}$ 1	3 4 $\bar{5}$ 1
1 $\bar{5}$ 3 1	3 1 $\bar{5}$ 4 3 2 1	1 3 $\bar{5}$ 1	5 $\bar{5}$ 4 $\bar{5}$ 3 2 1
1 $\bar{5}$ 3 4 3 1	3 $\bar{5}$ 4 3 2 1	1 3 4 $\bar{5}$ 1	5 4 $\bar{5}$ 3 2 1
1 $\bar{5}$ 4 3 1	5 3 1 $\bar{5}$ 4 3 1	1 3 5 3 4 $\bar{5}$ 1	5 3 4 $\bar{5}$ $\bar{6}$ $\bar{7}$ 1
1 $\bar{7}$ $\bar{6}$ $\bar{5}$ 4 3 2 1	5 $\bar{5}$ 4 3 2 1	1 5 4 $\bar{5}$ 1	1 2 3 4 $\bar{5}$ $\bar{6}$ $\bar{7}$ 1

(3) 6/8 Meter.   Tap the following and intone the rhythm.   (a)

Repeat, dividing each pulse into triplets.   (b)

As a six-pulse meter is a compound of a duple meter, each pulse divided into triplets, compare the following exercises with the above. Tap the pulse as in 2/4, and intone.

In beating 6/8 meter in a moderate or fast tempo, beat as in duple meter: down, up, ↓1 ↑2 mentally dividing each pulse into three.

In beating 6/8 in a slow tempo, beat as follows: one down; two beats to the left; two beats to the right; one up.   2 ← ↓1 ↑6 → 5   3   4

For use in these lessons, beat as a duple meter.

Practise the following; beat 1 2, and intone the rhythm.

(4) *Phrases for Dictation containing* 5̄ 4; 4 5̄:

(a) Outline rhythm—two dots in a measure:

representing the pulses. As the phrase is played, place pencil on dot as the pulse recurs and decide the number of notes to the pulse. If there are three, place 3 under the dot.

Number 2 would be outlined

(b) Pitches are dictated and outlined in the usual manner.

NOTE. In harmonizing phrases in 6/8 for dictation, use an accompaniment which will give two pulses in each measure. Number 8 might be played thus:

Section C.

1 (a) Contrast the following exercises, beating 1 2.

(b) Practise the following; beat 1 2, and intone rhythm.

(2) *Exercises in Sight-Singing:*

CHAPTER X

Chords

A *Chord* is three, four or five tones placed one above the other in *thirds;* all the tones to be sounded at the same time.

The tone upon which the chord is built is the *Root* of the chord.

The next tone is the *third*, the next the *fifth*, the next the *seventh*, the next the *ninth* of the chord.* Each tone is named from its interval-relationship to the root of the chord.

A three-tone chord is a *Triad.* A four-tone chord is a *Chord of the Seventh* (seventh-chord).

Triad. Chord of the 7th. Chord of the 9th

A five-tone chord is a *Chord of the Ninth.*

A chord may be built upon each tone of a key.

A chord is named from the degree of the scale which is used as its root. If the root is the first degree of the scale, it is a *One Chord* (I), or *Tonic Chord;* if the fifth degree, a *Five Chord* (V), or *Dominant Chord;* etc.

Roman numerals are used as symbols of chords.

Most chords are triads with a duplication one octave higher of one of the tones, generally the root. The *tonic chord* is 1, 3, 5, 8; the *dominant chord*, 5, 7, 2, 5; the *subdominant chord*, 4, 6, 8, 4; the *two-chord* 2, 4, 6, 2; the *six-chord*, 6, 8, 3, 6; the *three-chord*, 3, 5, 7, 3.

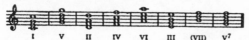

I   V   II   IV   VI   III   (VII)   V⁷

The I, V and IV chords consist of a major 3rd and a perfect 5th from the root. These chords are *major chords.* The II, VI and III chords consist of a minor 3rd and a perfect 5th from the root. These chords are *minor chords.* The VII chord consists of a minor 3rd and a diminished 5th from the root. As this chord upon seven is imperfect, i. e., the only chord with a diminished 5th, and is included in and used as the seventh-chord built upon the dominant, it is not considered, by most theorists, as an independent triad.

A chord is major or minor according to the size of its third.

'In this connection the 9th is an independent interval.

LESSON 18

Section A.

Suggestions for Study:

NOTE. As chords are used in this book only in broken form in melodic construction, not as in four-part chord-writing, these exercises are to be written in the treble, in close position.

(1) Erect the I, V, II, IV, VI, III chords in every major key, using signatures.

(2) Learn the quality of the chords in a *major key*. The I, V and IV chords are *major*; the II, VI and III chords are *minor*.

(3) Learn to recite rapidly the numbers of the scale-degrees which make up the chords. Example: The I chord, 1, 3, 5, 8; the V chord, 5, 7, 2, 5; etc.

(4) Reduce the tones in each measure to thirds and name the chord:

Section B.

(1) Review the intervals of Lesson 16, Section C, page 92. Add the following:

(2) (a) Play the tonic chord of every major key.

(b) Hold down the keys (of the chord) and sing as an arpeggio: 1 3 5 8 ; 8 5 3 1.

(c) Hold down the keys and sing, first by number, then by letter, the root, third, fifth and octave.

(3) *Melodies for Dictation and Sight-Singing:*

In outlining the rhythm ♩ ♪ in ⁶⁄₈ write a 2 under the dot. This is the only combination of two notes on a pulse in 6/8. Number 2 would be outlined ⁶⁄₈ ³₃ ³₃ | ²₂ · | ²₂ ²₂ | ‿ ‖

The figure ♩ ♪ is easily recognized as a limping or lame figure.

Section C.

(1) Practice of the up-beat in 6/8 meter. Arm-movement.

I₁ I² Tap the beat and intone rhythm.

(a) ♩. ♩ ♪ ♫♫♩ ♪ ♩. ♩ ♩ ♩. ♩. ‖ Contrast with ♪ ♩. ♩ ♩ ♪ ♫♫♩ ♪ ♩. ♩ ♩ ♩. ♩ ‖

(b) ♫♫♫♩ ♩ ♩ ♩ ♩ ♩. ♫♫ ♩ ♩. ♩. ‖ " " ♪ ♫♫ ♫♫ ♩ ♩ ♩ ♩ ♩. ♫♫ ♩ ♩. ♩ ‖

(c) ♩ ♪♫♫ ♩ ♩ ♪♫♫ ♫♫♩ ♩ ♩ ♩. ♩. ‖ " " ♪ ♩ ♪♫♫ ♩ ♩ ♪♫♫ ♫♫♩ ♩ ♩ ♩. ‖

(d) ♫♫♩ ♪ ♫♫♩ ♩ ♩ ♩. ♫♫ ♩ ♩. ‖ " " ♪ ♫♫♩ ♪ ♫♫♩ ♩ ♩ ♩. ♫♫ ♩ ♩ ‖

(2) *Exercises in Sight-Singing:*

E. German

A.S. Sullivan

Mendelssohn

Lesson 19

In Minor, chords are erected in the same manner as in major. The quality of the chords is different, because of the lowering of the third and sixth degrees.

The I and IV chords have a minor 3rd and perfect 5th, and are *Minor Chords*.

The V and VI chords have a major 3rd and perfect 5th, and are *Major Chords*.

The II chord has a minor 3rd and diminished 5th, and is a *Diminished Chord*.

The III chord has a major 3rd and augmented 5th, and is an *Augmented Chord*.

Illustration: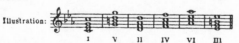

NOTE. The III chord is seldom used in major or minor.

A chord is diminished or augmented according to the size of its fifth.

A *Seventh-Chord*, i. e., a chord of four different tones, may be built upon each tone of the key except I. The seventh-chord upon I is questionable. All seventh-chords demand that another chord shall follow to make them complete, and as the I chord is the key-centre and must give a feeling of rest, we should not kill this feeling by adding a seventh.

The *seventh-chords* built upon V and II are the most used. V⁷ and II⁷ are symbols of these chords.

The most used *ninth-chord* is the one built upon V, the V⁹ chord. This chord is most satisfactory when the root is omitted, ₀V⁹.

Section A.

Suggestions for Study:

(1) Erect the I, V, II, IV, VI and III chords in every minor key. (See illustration, p. 105.)

(2) Learn the quality of the chords in minor (the I and IV, minor, etc.).

(3) Erect a V⁷ and II⁷ chord in every key. Learn the numbers of the scale-degrees which make these chords.

(4) Erect a V⁹ chord in every key. Learn the numbers of the scale-degrees which make this chord.

(5) Each of the following measures consists of the tones of some chord in the key of D major.

Reduce to chord-formation and name the chord.

(6) Play first the I, then the V, then the I chord in every major key.

Play first the I, then the IV, then the I chord in every major key.

Play first the I, then the IV, then the V then the I chord in every major key.

(7) Repeat the same in minor.

(8) Learn the names of the pitches of the tonic, dominant and subdominant chords in every key.

Section B.

(1) Review the Intervals of Lesson 16, Section C, page 92, and Lesson 18, Section B, page 102.

Add the following:

(2) (a) Play the tonic chord in every minor key.

(b) Hold down the keys (of the chord) and sing as an arpeggio 1 3 5 8; 8 5 3 1.

(c) Hold down the keys and sing, first by letter, then by number, the root, third, fifth and octave.

(3) *Phrases for Dictation and Singing:*

NOTE. A phrase in compound meter seems to subdivide into two equal sections. In singing the phrase it is generally a necessary to take quick or "catch" breath between these sections. In memorizing the phrase the mind should divide it into two sections, as the breath demands in singing. Phrases which are impossible to remember in one section can be easily retained by taking a mental catch breath. The mind does not easily retain a passage which is longer than that which the average singer can sing in one breath. This is the foundation of phrasing in music.

Section C.

(1) Review the rhythmic exercises of Lessons 18, Section C, page 103; 17, Section C, page 98; and 15, Section B, page 86.

(2) Practise rhythms while walking about the room, taking a step for each pulse and intoning the figures, subdividing and adding the pulses.

(3) *Exercises in Sight-Singing:*

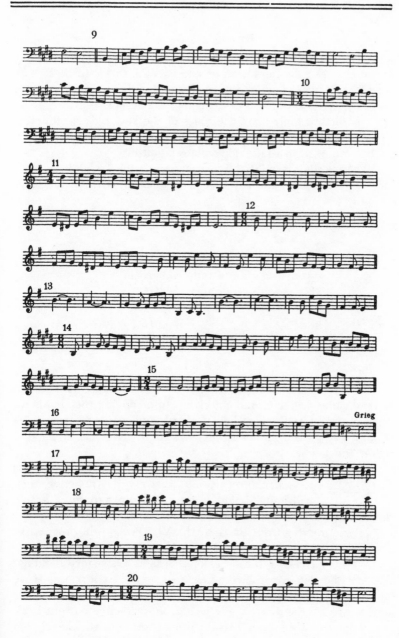

Chords are used in music to establish keys and to give accents. The progression or resolution of one chord into another gives an accent. The chord upon the unaccented pulse resolves into the chord upon the accented pulse, making the accent.

Chords are built upon the tones of the key, i. e., the different pitches found by dividing a string into thirds, and not upon these pitches arranged in the major scale relationship.

The chords are related and progress to the I chord, as these tones are related to the key-tone. If we begin with C, the tones

of the key are:

These tones as roots
of chords and arranged in
this order are: III

VI

II

V

I

IV

As we progress away from C, the tones become less active; as they come nearer C, more active. In arranging the chords we transpose the position of the IV chord, and place it between the II and VI, as the II^7 chord includes the tones of the IV, and is nearer the key-centre.

We begin with the I chord, and may progress to any chord. As all other chords are active, they will immediately begin to progress to more active chords until they come to rest on the I chord.

If we progress from the I to the VI, the VI will progress to some chord nearer the centre, the IV, II or V, and then to the I.

We may consider the series of chords as a six-story building. We take the elevator from the first floor to the sixth floor. If we jump from the window we move down, going faster and faster until we reach the ground. It would be impossible to turn back at any point. We go from I to any other chord, but all other chords must progress to a chord nearer the centre of the key.

The V and IV chords are the only chords which may progress immediately into the I. The other chords will pass through V or IV before going to I. The III always goes to IV or II before going to V.

There are many exceptions to these progressions, but the fundamental progressions are most used and should be thoroughly learned before exceptions are attempted.

CHAPTER XI

Melody—Regular Scale-Line and Narrow Skips

A *Melody* is a succession of single related tones. A melody must have form and rhythmic variety.

A melody should be smooth or legato. As stepwise or diatonic progression is the smoothest progression in music, a melody may progress up or down a major scale.

In a major scale there are rest tones and active tones. All active tones resolve to the nearest rest tones. Fundamentally, all active tones in a melody should resolve. Theoretically, the progression 3 4 5 is not possible, as 4 must resolve to 3; 5 6 7 8, as 6 must resolve to 5; 8 7 6 5, as 7 must resolve to 8; but see Chapter XII.

A tone may be repeated usually not more than five times; although two or three repetitions are enough. Repetitions give poise to a melody.

Next to stepwise or scale progression, the skip of a third is the smoothest progression.

From the rest tones the jump of a third may be made in either direction. If the jump is made to an active tone, it must resolve. In jumping from 5 to 7, 7 will resolve to 8.

From the active tones jumps are naturally made in the direction of their resolution—up from 7, down from 6 or 4, and either way from 2.

Only one skip of a third will be made in the same direction. The jump of a third from a tone and immediately back to the tone may be made, as 1 3 1.

These are the fundamental laws which govern simple melodic movement. From these, or by breaking these laws, we learn to use the more interesting melodic movements.

In literature sentences of different construction are used as forms in which to express a complete thought. In music there are similar forms. The smallest form expressing a complete thought is a *phrase*.

A melody in phrase-form may be of any length. When regular, it is four measures. A phrase may begin on an accented or unaccented pulse, with any tone of the tonic chord, i. e., 1, 3, 5 or 8. A phrase must end on an accented pulse of the fourth measure, with the key-tone, 1 or 8, preceded by some tone of the dominant chord, 5, 7 or 2. If the meter is duple or triple, it will end on the first pulse. In a compound meter, it will end on either the primary or secondary accent. This ending or close is a *Perfect Authentic Cadence*.

A melody may also end on either 3 or 5, but the effect is incomplete and is equivalent to a question-mark in punctuation.

As a summary: fundamentally, if a melody is correct:

(1) All active tones will resolve, therefore the progressions 3 4 5, 5 6 7 8, 8 7 6 5, cannot be used.

(2) A tone may be repeated two or three times.

(3) From rest tones jumps of a third are made in either direction.

(4) From active tones jumps of a third are made in the direction of their resolution.

(5) A melody may begin on an accented or unaccented pulse with 1, 3, 5 or 8.

(6) A melody will end on an accented pulse of the fourth measure with 1 or 8, preceded by 7 or 2.

(7) The melody will be a four-measure phrase in length.

LESSON 20

Section A.

Suggestions for Study:

(1) Write a melody in each major key, employing the fundamental laws given above. Use the following meters: 2/2, 2/4, 3/2, 3/4, 3/8, 4/4, 4/2, 6/8, 6/4. Make the rhythm uniform, i. e., a note for each pulse except in the last measure. Use an added beat to the last measure.

(2) How to write melody. Rule four measures on the staff. If the meter is to be 3/4 and the rhythm begins on the accent, make three dots under each measure to represent the pulses. On the first pulse write, 1 3 5 8. As this is a simple meter, the melody

must end on the first pulse of the fourth measure. Place 1 and 8 on that pulse. On the pulse preceding, 5, 7 or 2 must be used to make a cadence. The fifth degree cannot be used, as the jump from 5 to 8 is larger than a 3rd. Begin with any tone, 1 3 5 8, and progress according to the above laws and arrange the tones one on each pulse, having the melody end so that either 7 or 2 goes to 8. You might begin with 5, use 6 on the next pulse, which must progress to 5, repeat 5, jump to 7, which should resolve to 8, jump to 3, come back to 2, jump to 7, which resolves to 8.

In the same way, if the melody is written in 4/4, beginning on the up-beat and ending on the secondary accent. Make the outline first, then write the tune. 6/8 is constructed in the same manner.

Section B.

(1) Review the Intervals of Lessons 16, Section C, page 92; 18, Section B, page 102; and 19, Section B, page 107.

Add the following:

(2) Unrelated or Absolute Intervals.—Major and Minor Thirds.

(a) Play each of the intervals of (1) and sing (1 3) (Major 3rd).
    Play the lower tone, sing the upper.
    Play the upper tone, sing the lower.
(b) Play each of the intervals of (2) and sing 3 5 (Minor 3rd).
    Play the lower tone, sing the upper.
    Play the upper tone, sing the lower.
(c) Play each of the intervals of (3) and determine if it is a major or a minor 3rd, testing if it is 1 3 or 3 5.

(3) Review the chords of Lessons 18, Section B, page 102, and 19, Section B, page 107.

(a) Play the Dominant (V) Chord in every Major Key.

(b) Hold down the keys and sing as an arpeggio 5 7 2 5; 5 2 7 5.

(c) Hold down the keys and sing, first by letter, then by number, the root, third, fifth and octave.

(4) *Melodies for Dictation and Singing,* containing progressions allowed in Lesson 20, Section A, page 113.

These melodies are to be dictated, outlined and written in the usual manner.

Section C.

(1) Review Lesson 19, Section C (1) and (2), page 108.

(2) *Exercises in Sight-Singing:*

Folk-Song

CHAPTER XII

Melody—Irregular Scale-Line and Narrow Skips

Fundamentally, active tones have to resolve, but they may be forced in the wrong direction by progressing along the scale. The progressions 8 7 6 5, 5 6 7 8, and 3 4 5, are permissible because in each of these progressions the scale-line and the pitch of the first and last tones is heard, and not the character of the separate tones.

In progressing up or down a scale, if the melody stops, turns back, or repeats a tone, the scale-line is broken. The tone at which the break is made is brought into prominence. If this tone is a rest tone, there is nothing involved. If it is an active tone, it must resolve. In progressing up the scale, the melody may turn at any tone except 7, which, because of its own upward tendency, is forced to proceed to 8. In progressing down the scale, the melody may turn at any tone but six or four, which are similarly on the way down and will have to continue.

Fundamentally, jumps of a third are made, from active tones, only in the direction of their resolution. Jumps of a third in the other direction, i. e., down from 7, up 6 or 4, are possible, but the melody must turn back immediately.

After a jump of a third from an active tone, contrary to the direction of its resolution, the melody may, first, return along the scale and resolve the active tone, e. g., 7 5 6 7 8; second, it may jump back to the active tone and resolve it, 7 5 7 8; third, it may turn back for one tone and progress down the scale, 7 5 6 5 4 3. The same applies to the other active tones.

7 5 6 7 8   7 5 7 8   7 5 6 5 4 3

LESSON 21

Section A.

Suggestions for Study:
(1) Write a melody in each major key, using 3/2, 3/4, 3/8, 4 ′4, 4/2, 6/4 and 6/8 meters. Rhythm uniform, in the same manner as in the preceding lesson, but forcing the active scale-degrees in

the wrong direction, i. e., using the progressions 3 4 5; 5 6 7 8; 8 7 6 5; and jumping a third up from 6 or 4, and down from 7.

Section B.

(1) Review the Intervals of Lessons 16, Section C, page 92; 18, Section B, page 102; 19, Section B, page 107; and 20, Section B, page 114.

(2) Absolute Intervals : Perfect Fifth and Perfect Fourth.

(a) Play each of the intervals of (a) and sing 1 5 (Perf. 5th).
   Play the lower tone, sing the upper.
   Play the upper tone, sing the lower.

(b) Play each of the intervals of (b) and sing 5 8 (Perf. 4th).
   Play the lower tone, sing the upper.
   Play the upper tone, sing the lower.

(c) Play each of the intervals, of (c) and determine if it is a perfect 5th or a perfect 4th, testing if it is 1 5 or 5 8.

(3) (a) Review the chords of Lessons 18, Section B, page 102; 19, Section B, page 107; and 20, Section B, page 115.

(b) Play the Dominant Chord, followed by the Tonic Chord, in every Major key.

Major key

(c) Sing in every key, with numbers and letter-names:
   5 7 2 5, 1 3 5 8;   5 7 2 5, 8 5 3 1
   5 2 7 5, 8 5 3 1;   5 2 7 5, 1 3 5 8

(4) *Melodies for Dictation and Singing*, containing progressions allowed in Lesson 21, Section A:

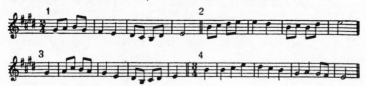

Section C.

(1) *Rhythmic Drill.* ♪♪♪♪ in $\frac{2}{4}$ and $\frac{3}{4}$

(a) Beat the meter; think the rhythm, then intone the rhythm.

(b) Walk the meter, then intone the rhythm.

(2) *Exercises in Sight-Singing:*

CHAPTER XIII

Melody—Wide Skips

Any skip larger than a third is a *wide* skip. Skips of all intervals are made, though a skip beyond an octave is rare.

All skips must be between tones of a chord. The jump from 1 to 7 or 7 to 1 is not good, as there is no 7th in the I chord. The skip from 3 up to 7 or from 7 down to 3 is not used, as it is part of the III chord, which is so far from the key-centre that these skips sound as if in a new key.

After every wide skip the melody will turn and progress in the other direction, preferably along the scale. It may continue along the scale in the same direction for two or three tones, and then turn. Wide skips are better made within the measure, and not over the bar.

In jumping to active tones it is better to jump from above to 7, and from below to 6 or 4, so that the melody will turn after the wide leap and at the same time resolve the active tones. If a wide skip is made to 7 from below, or to 6 or 4 from above, the melody may turn and leave the active tone unresolved, as the necessity for turning after a wide skip counteracts the demand for resolution of the active tone.

A wide skip may be made in either direction *from a rest tone*, and to any tone except the progressions given above (1 7 and 3 7).

The natural direction in which to jump *from active tones* is in the direction of their resolution. All skips up from 7 and down from 6 and 4 are correct.

A skip may be made down from 7. The only skips which sound well are 7 to 5, and 7 to 2.

A skip may be made up from 4 or 6 to any tone.

The most beautiful melodies possess skips of a third, an occasional wide skip, repeated tones and a predominance of scale-progression.

The resolution of active tones may be deferred, as long as they are resolved after three or four tones. We may progress 5 4 5 if it is followed by 3, 2 3 or 1 2 3. Also 5 6 7 5 8 or 5 6 7 5 2 8, or 5 6 7 5 3 2 8.

The ear will wait during the passing of three or four tones for an active tone to resolve, but will never feel satisfied unless it eventually does resolve.   Thus:

5 4 5 3   5 4 5 2 3   5 4 5 1 2 3   5 6 7 5 8   5 6 7 5 2 8   5 6 7 5 3 2 1

LESSON 22

Section A.

Suggestions for Study:

(1) Write a melody in each major key in the same manner as in previous lessons and use an occasional wide skip.

Section B.

(1) Review the Intervals of Lessons 16, Section C, page 92; 18, Section B, page 102; 19, Section B, page 107; 20, Section B, page 114; and 21, Section B, page 119.

(2) Absolute Intervals.   The Minor 6th.

(a) Play each of the intervals of (a) and sing 3 8 (minor 6th).
Play the lower tone, sing the upper.
Play the upper tone, sing the lower.

(b) As the minor 6th is often confused with the perfect 4th, play each of the intervals of (a) followed by the perfect 4th in the same key, as outlined in (b). Sing 3 8 (minor 6th), 5 8 (perfect 4th).   Compare the difference in quantity and quality.

(c) Play each of the intervals of (c) and determine if it is a minor 6th or perfect 4th, testing if it is 3 8 or 5 8.

(3) Review the chords of Lessons 18, Section B, page 102; 19, Section B, page 107; 20, Section B, page 115; and 21, Section B, page 119.

(4) *Melodies for Dictation and Singing*, containing progressions allowed in Lesson 22, Section A and ♩♩♩♩ in ²⁄₄ and ³⁄₄

NOTE. In outlining the rhythm ♩♩♩♩ in $\frac{2}{4}$ and $\frac{3}{4}$ write 4 under the pulse.

No. 1 $\frac{2}{4}$ ♩ ♩ |♩ · |♩ ♩ '⌣ ♪

Harmonize the ♩♩♩♩ with one chord.

In memorizing pitches do not try to remember the numbers or the first tone. Relax and listen to the entire tune. After two or three playings it should be retained by the mind, so that it can be sung and analyzed. Determine the construction and general outline of the melody, whether scale-line or skips are used. Look at the rhythmic outline and determine upon which pulses these occur.

Number 1 would be analyzed thus: 1st measure, scale-line from 1 to 5 on first pulse of the 2nd measure; 2nd measure, repetition of 5 6; 3rd measure, wide skip 5 to rest tone 8; scale-line back to 5, and then cadence 2 1.

Section C.

(1) *Rhythmic drill for* ♩♫♫ *in* 4/4 *and* ♩♫♫♫ *in* 6/8

(a) Beat the meter; think the rhythm; intone the rhythm.

(b) Walk the meter, intone the rhythm.

(2) *Exercises in Sight-Singing:*

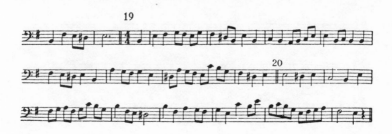

CHAPTER XIV

Melody—Consecutive Skips

Any *consecutive* skips in the same direction in a melody must be between tones of a chord.

From 1 we can use, theoretically, only the tones 1, 3, 5, 8 (I chord or 1 4 6 8 (IV chord); rarely 1 3 6 8 (VI chord).

From 5 we can use, theoretically, only the tones 5, 7, 2, 4, 6 (V^9 chord), or 5 1 3 5 (I chord).

From 4 we can use, theoretically, only the tones 4, 6, 8, or rarely 3 (IV^7 chord), or 4 6 2 4 (II chord).

From 2 we can use, theoretically, only the tones 2, 4, 6, 8 (II^7 chord), or 2 5 7 2 (V chord).

From 6 we can use, theoretically, only the tones 6, 8, 3, rarely 5 (VI^7 chord), or 6 2 4 6 (II chord).

From 7 we can use, theoretically, only the tones 7, 2, 4, 5, 6 (V^9 chord).

From 3 we can use, theoretically, only the tones 3, 5, 8, (I chord), 3, 6, 1 (VI chord).

Consecutive skips in the same direction are made for one measure, one-half measure, or one pulse.

Consecutive skips are not continued beyond the bar, as this keeps the same chord, and chords must change over the bar to give an accent.

Consecutive skips are generally followed by scale-line, or single wide or narrow skips in the opposite direction. (After consecutive skips, skips in the other direction are dangerous, because they are apt to give poor chord-progression. This will be avoided by using the scale-line for three or four tones.)

LESSON 23

Section A.

Suggestions for Study:
(1) Write a melody in each major key, employing the meters and constructions of the previous lessons, adding consecutive skips in the same direction.

Section B.

(1) Review the intervals of Lessons 16, Section C, page 92; 18, Section B, page 102; 19, Section B, page 107; 20, Section B, page 114; 21, Section B, page 119; and 22, Section B, page 124; and add A♭ major.

(2) Absolute Intervals.   The Major 6th.

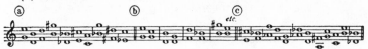

(a) Play each of the intervals of (a) and sing 5 $\underline{3}$ (Major 6th).
Play the lower tone, sing the upper.
Play the upper tone, sing the lower.

(b) As the major 6th is often confused with the perfect 4th, play each of the intervals of (a) followed by the perfect 4th in the same key, as outlined in (b). Sing 5 $\underline{3}$ (Major 6th), 5 8 (Perfect 4th). Compare the difference in quantity and quality.

(c) Play each of the intervals of (c) and determine if it is a major 6th or a perfect 4th, testing if it is 5 $\underline{3}$ or 5 8.

(3) (a) Review the chords of the preceding lessons.

(b) Play the dominant seventh-chord (V⁷) in each major key, followed by the tonic chord:

(c) Sing the V⁷ chord in arpeggio form in each major key: 5 7 2 4, followed by 3 1.

(4) *Melodies for Dictation and Singing*, containing progressions of Lesson 23, Section A and ♪♪♪♪ in $\frac{4}{4}$ and ♪♪♪♪♪♪ in $\frac{6}{8}$

NOTE: In outlining the rhythm ♪♪♪♪ in 4/4 with 4 under pulse.

In outlining the rhythm ♪♪♪♪♪♪ in 6/8 with 6 under pulse.

Section C.

(1) Review rhythmic drill of Lessons 21, Section C, page 120; and 22, Section C, page 126.

(2) *Exercises in Sight-Singing:*

CHAPTER XV

Minor Melody

We have seen that the minor scale is made by lowering the third and sixth degrees of the major scale. In the same way any major melody may be made minor by lowering its third and sixth degrees.

A *minor melody* may be written with the proper minor signature, which is borrowed from the major key of the same name as the third degree. When using the minor signature the seventh degree has to be raised by an accidental.

Minor melodies are constructed in the same manner as major melodies. In a minor scale the progression from 6 to 7 is an Augmented 2nd. An augmented 2nd sounds like a minor 3rd, which is a skip. If the scale-progression 5 6 7 8 is seen on the paper, we expect to hear the smooth diatonic progression of major and minor 2nds. In minor, when using the progressions 5 6 7 8 or 8 7 6 5, we hear the jump of the augmented 2nd, while the eye sees a scale. In order to overcome this discrepancy and make the progression sound diatonic, the 6th *degree* is *raised* when it progresses up to 7, and the 7th *degree* is *lowered* when it progresses down to 6:

NOTE. To avoid confusion, remember that in thinking and writing in minor the 7th is always raised, as the minor signature lowers the 3rd, 6th, and 7th degrees of the major scale.

In studying the above, remember that you help 6 up to 7 by raising it, and 7 down to 6 by lowering it.

This results in what is known as the *Melodic Form* of the Minor Scale. It is a modification of the Harmonic Form, and is used only in melodic progression when 6 goes up to 7, or 7 down to 6.

The following are exceptions: The form with the lowered 7th is used in the ascending scale-line, when the IV, II or VI chord is used for the harmonization. The raised form of the scale would clash with the tones of the chord. For the same reason, the form with the raised 6th is used in the descending scale-line when the V chord is used for the harmonization.

In making a wide skip down to 6 and progressing back along the scale up to 8, the raised form is used if the chord impression is the V. If it is the IV, the lowered form is used. In making a skip from any tone up to 7 and progressing down the scale, the raised form is used, as the chord impression is always the V.

The Augmented 2nd is retained while jumping in the V chord. For example, the following appears to have a scale-progression, 7 6 5 4, but it is in reality an arpeggio, formed from the tones of the V⁹ chord, and affects the ear as such.

LESSON 24

Section A.

Suggestions for Study:

(1) Transpose six of the major melodies of the last lesson into the Parallel Minor Key. In each case, change to the minor signature and raise the 7th degree. If there are any 6th degrees going up to 7, raise the 6th as well. If there are 7th degrees going down to 6, lower the 7th.

(2) Construct six new melodies in minor. Use occasionally the progressions 6 7 8 and 8 7 6.

Section B.

(1) Review the intervals of the preceding lessons.

(2) Absolute Intervals. Comparison of Major and Minor Sixths.

(a) Review carefully Lesson 22, Section B (2), page 124, and Lesson 23, Section B (2), page 130.

(b) Play each of the intervals of (a) and determine if it is a Major or Minor 6th, testing if it is 5 <u>3</u> or 3 8.

(3) Review the chords of the preceding lesson.

(4) *Melodies for Dictation and Singing:*

Minor melodies are to be dictated the same as the major melodies.

Section C.

(1) *Rhythmic Study:* ♩♫ in $\frac{2}{4}$ and $\frac{3}{4}$

(2) Exercises in Sight-Singing:

CHAPTER XVI

Regular and Irregular Rhythms

Rhythm is *regular* when the longer notes occupy the accented pulses of the meter. It is irregular when the shorter notes occupy the accented pulses of the meter.

Following is a table of divided and added pulses of a regular quarter-note rhythm in duple and triple meter. All additions and subdivisions in half and eighth-note rhythms are in proportion.

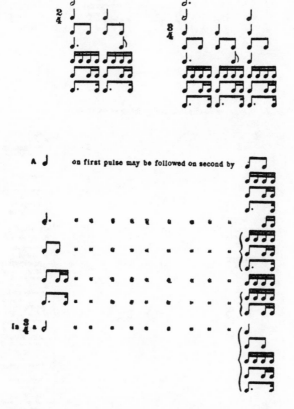

4/4 corresponds to 2/4 with the addition of a ♩ and ♩. on the first pulse.

Following is a table of divided and added beats of a regular eighth-note rhythm in a six-pulse meter.

A 𝅘𝅥𝅮. on first pulse may be followed on second by

Outline of Melody-Writing

Scale-Line
  I. Rest Tones.
 II. Active Tones.

   (a) Must resolve.
   (b) May be forced along
       scale-line.
       1. In progressing up,
          do not turn at 7.
       2. In progressing
          down, do not turn
          at 6 or 4.
   (c) Force after wide skip.
   (d) Force by using con-
       secutive skips.
   (e) Delay resolution.
III. Minor.

   (a) Lower 3rd and 6th of
       major.
   (b) 6 to 7, raise 6: 7 to 6,
       lower 7.

Skips
  I. A 3rd (a narrow skip).
   (a) From Rest Tones.
       1. Both directions.
   (b) From Active Tones.

       1. In direction of reso-
          lution.
       2. Contrary to direc-
          tion of regular resolu-
          tion.
          (a) Must turn.

 II. Single wide skips.
   (a) Must be part of a chord.
   (b) Must turn.
III. Consecutive skips.
   (a) Must spell a chord.
   (b) Conform to the meter.
   (c) Must turn.

LESSON 25

Section A.

Suggestions for Study:

(1) Construct twelve melodies in minor, using duple or triple
meter and any of the regular rhythms given in Chapter XVI.

(2) Learn the outline of Melody-Writing.

Section B.

(1) Absolute Intervals:

(a) Play each interval: listen to its sound, determine its
quantity and quality; test by singing numbers.

(2) Intervals in a Minor Key:

(a) Rewrite all the intervals of Lesson 16, Section C, page 91, in the parallel minor key.

(b) Learn the difference in the position of the Major and Minor 6th and 3rd in a Minor key: 1 3 a Minor 3rd, 3 5 a Major 3rd, 3 8 a Major 6th; 5 3̲ a Minor 6th.

(c) Practise in the same manner as in major.

(3) Practise chords as in the preceding lessons, using both major and minor modes.

(4) *Melodies for Dictation and Singing*, employing ♩♫

NOTE. In outlining rhythms there are two figures of three notes which fall on one pulse; the triplet, and ♫♪ expressed "

For these exercises all consecutive skips in the same direction are in the tonic chord.

(a) Follow directions for pitch analysis given in Lesson 22, Section B, page 124.

Section C.

(1) *Rhythmic Study:* ♪♫ in $\frac{4}{4}$ and ♩ ♫ in $\frac{6}{8}$

(2) *Exercises in Sight-Singing:*

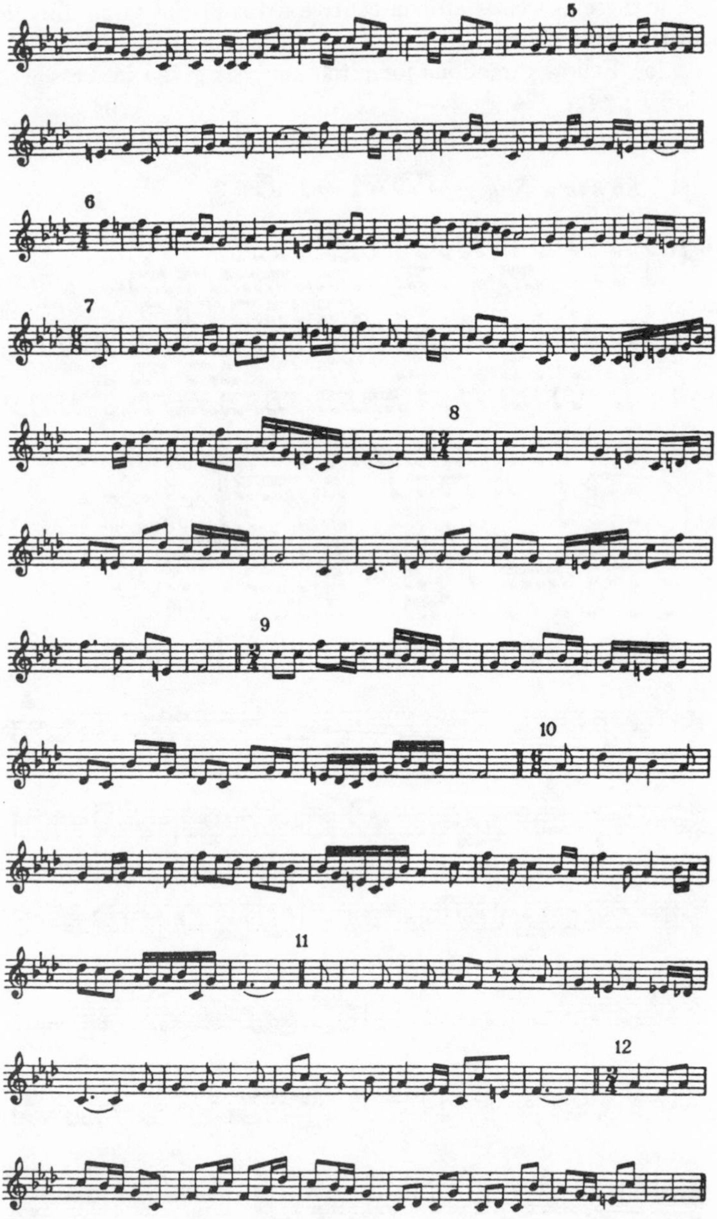
5
6
7
8
9
10
11
12

CHAPTER XVII
Period-Form

A phrase in music corresponds to a simple sentence in English. In English we often use a compound sentence, which is in reality two sentences, one qualifying the other, each expressing a thought. In music a *Period* corresponds to this form.

A Period, when regular, consists of two phrases, each usually four measures long. The first is the *Antecedent Phrase*, the second the *Consequent Phrase*. A period begins as any phrase, but the antecedent phrase ends with some tone of the V-chord, 5, 7 or 2, instead of 1 or 8. This gives the effect of being incomplete, and makes a *Semi-Cadence*. The consequent phrase ends with 1 or 8, a *Perfect Authentic Cadence*.

A Period is in *Parallel Construction* when at least the first measure of the antecedent and that of the consequent phrase are alike.

There are three stages of parallel construction:

(1) When the *first three* measures of the consequent phrase are like the first three measures of the antecedent phrase, the cadence alone being changed.

(2) When the *first two* measures of the antecedent and the consequent phrase are the same.

(3) When the *first* measure of the antecedent is the same as the first measure of the consequent phrase.

Lesson 26
Parallel Construction
Section A.

Suggestions for Study:

(1) Construct six periods in parallel construction. For each antecedent phrase make three consequent phrases, one of each stage. (See model below.)

Section B.

(1) Review the Absolute Intervals of the preceding lessons.

(2) Continue the study of intervals in minor as outlined in Lesson 25, Section B, page 142.

(3) The intervals used in a key have been between the tones 1 3 5 8, which is the Tonic Chord.

The Major 3rd, 1 – 3, from the Root to the Third of the chord.

The Minor 3rd, 3 – 5, from the Third to the Fifth of the chord.

The Major 6th, 5 – 3, from the Fifth to the Third of the chord.

The Minor 6th, 3 – 8, from the Third to the Eighth of the chord.

The Perfect 5th, 1 – 5, from the Root to the Fifth of the chord.

The Perfect 4th, 5 – 8, from the Fifth to the Eighth of the chord.

Harmonic, and most Melodic Intervals, are *parts of a chord* and sound in relation to the *Root* of the chord.

Since the I, V and IV chords are major chords, their interval content is the same.

As these chords are used in composition, the same intervals occur between different scale-degrees.

In the V, or Dominant Chord:	In the IV, or Subdom. Chord:
Major 3rd, Root to Third, from 5th–7th degrees	from the 4th–6th degrees
Minor 3rd, Third to Fifth, from 7th–2nd degrees	from the 6th–8th degrees
Major 6th, Fifth to Third, from 2nd–7th degrees	from the 1st–6th degrees
Minor 6th, Third to Eighth, from 7th–5th degrees	from the 6th–4th degrees
Perfect 5th, Root to Fifth, from 5th–2nd degrees	from the 4th–8th degrees
Perfect 4th, Fifth to Eighth, from 2nd–5th degrees	from the 1st–4th degrees

All these intervals are *consonant* intervals, or intervals which are complete and do not need resolution. As they occur in the I chord there is no question as to their position in the key. As different chords are used and four or five intervals occur in a chord, other than the I chord, there is a danger, because of their consonant quality, of losing the feeling of the active and inactive scale-degrees, or the key-centre. This cannot happen if the change of chord is recognized and the position of the intervals in the chord is known. For example, in this series the first three intervals, a Major 3rd, 1 3, a Perfect 5th, 1 5, a Minor 6th, 3 8, are known to be in the I (tonic) chord, as music generally begins with the I chord.

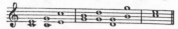

The next interval might be heard in the following ways:

(a) As a Major 3rd, but not in the I chord. If the new chord is recognized as the V chord, its position is known to be from the 5th to the 7th degree of the scale.

(b) If the scale-degrees 5 and 7 are recognized, it is known to be a Major 3rd and a part of the V chord.

(c) The 7th degree might be recognized as the upper tone of a Major third, so the interval is from the 5th to the 7th degree and in the V chord.

The next interval might be heard:

(d) As a Perfect 5th and in the same chord as the preceding interval, therefore from the 5th degree to the 2nd.

(e) If the scale-degrees 5 and 2 are heard, it is known to be a Perfect 5th in the V chord.

(f) It is more likely to sound I to 5, or Root to Fifth. This interval is felt to be a part of the same chord as the preceding interval, so it could not be from the 1st degree to the 5th, but from the Root to the Fifth of the V chord, and from the 5th degree to the 2nd.

The next interval, a Perfect 4th, will undoubtedly sound like 5 up to 1; the next, a Minor 6th, 3 up to 8. Unless we realize that these intervals are in the same chord as the two preceding and sound in relation to the root of that chord, the key-centre is lost. If they are known to be a Perfect 4th, from the 5th to the 1st (or Root), and a Minor 6th from the 3rd to the 8th of the V chord (*not* of the scale), they are easily placed in the key.

The last interval is heard as a Major 3rd in a different chord. As only the I chord can follow the V chord, the interval must be from 1 to 3.

(4) Learn the positions of the intervals in major chords, i. e., major 3rd from Root, Third, etc.

(5) Learn the position in the scale of the intervals in the V chord, i. e., Major 3rd from 5 to 7, etc.

(6) In each series (a) is in the I chord, (b) the V chord, and (c) the I chord.

(a) Practise (a) as before.   (b) Hear first the size of the interval, then place in the chord, then in the scale.

    (b) Play lower tone and sing the upper tone of each.

         Play upper tone and sing the lower tone of each.

    (c) Rewrite in the other keys and practise in same manner.

(7) Continue chord-practice in the same manner as in the preceding lessons.

(8) *Melodies for Dictation and Singing:*

(a) Play the entire tune.

(b) Name the form (Parallel Period).

(c) Decide the meter. (The meter is determined in Period-Form the same as in Phrase-Form, by the number of pulses in a phrase. Number 1 will be recognized as a period in 2/4 and not as a phrase in 4/4, because of the semi-cadence.)

(d) Dictate first the Antecedent Phrase in the usual manner, outlining rhythm, then pitches.

(e) Dictate Consequent Phrase. As these melodies are all Parallel, 1st stage, it will not be necessary to make a new outline; only change the cadence.

Section C.

(1) *Rhythmic Study:* $\frac{2}{4}$ ♩. ♪ – $\frac{3}{4}$ ♩. ♪♩

NOTE. In singing (a) ♩ ♩♫ or ♩. ♪ give a slight pressure on the second beat, so that the pulse is clearly defined. Exaggerate at first.

(2) *Exercises in Sight-Singing:*

Lesson 27

Contrasting Construction

A Period is in *Contrasting Construction* when the Consequent Phrase is different from the Antecedent.   Though the consequent phrase may be different, it will always be related to the antecedent in style and general construction.

Section A.

Suggestions for Study:

(1) Write six periods in contrasting construction; each of the six antecedent phrases to have three consequent phrases; thus:

Section B.

(1) Continue the practice of Absolute Intervals as in the preceding lessons.

(2) Review thoroughly Lesson 26, Section B (3), page 146.

(3) Practise the following intervals as outlined in the last lesson, page 148.

(4) Play the I–V⁷–I chords in every major key, as outlined.

(5) *Melodies for Dictation and Singing.*
Parallel Construction, 2nd stage, and Contrasting Construction: $\frac{2}{4}$ ♩. ♪, $\frac{3}{4}$ ♩. ♪♩

(a) Dictate one phrase at a time as in the preceding lesson. In these melodies it will be necessary to make a new outline for the consequent phrases. To outline the rhythm ♩. ♪ tie the two dots and place a check after 2nd dot. In No. 1, the first phrase would be outlined as follows:

Section C.

(1) *Rhythmic Study:* ♩. ♪ in 4/4

(2) *Exercises in Sight-Singing:*

CHAPTER XVIII

Figure or Motive. Exact Repetition and Sequence

A *Figure* in music is a group of notes arranged in a pattern, generally one measure long. A figure is used to express an idea from which is developed the complete thought, which makes a *phrase*. A figure makes a melody more comprehensive to the listener, because it permits of uniformity of design.

A figure is used in two ways: (1) In exact *repetition* when it is repeated on the same pitches; (2) in exact *sequence* when it is repeated on different pitches, the interval relationship of the tones remaining unchanged. More than one, or at most two, repetitions are seldom used at a time. There may be two or three sequences.

LESSON 28

Section A.

Suggestions for Study:

(1) Construct six Periods, three parallel, three contrasting; each antecedent to have three consequent phrases.

Develop each from a figure of one measure, used in exact sequence and repetition. Thus:

NOTE. In contrasting construction a new figure must be used for the consequent phrase. It may be similar to the first figure. (See example.)

Section B.

(1) Play F–G as an harmonic interval. Name it.

Notice that this interval needs something to make it complete, i. e., it needs resolution. Intervals which need resolution are *Dissonant Intervals.*

Play it again and note that the lower tone resolves down, while the upper tone is held:

[155]

Play G–F  as an harmonic interval.   Name it.

Notice that this interval also needs resolution; that the upper tone resolves down and the lower is held.

As an harmonic interval is part of a chord, the Minor 7th and its inversion must be part of a seventh-chord. The most used seventh-chord is the V⁷, therefore the Minor 7th is heard as $\bar{5}$ to 4 and the Major 2nd as 4 to 5, parts of that chord.

To distinguish the 2nd from the 7th; the lower tone of the 2nd resolves, and the upper tone of the 7th resolves.

(a) Play each of the intervals of (a) and sing 4–5 (Major 2nd).

     Play the lower tone, sing the upper.
     Play the upper tone, sing the lower and resolve it to 3.

(b) Play each of the intervals of (b) and sing $\bar{5}$–4 (Minor 7th).

     Play the lower tone, sing the upper and resolve it to 3.
     Play the upper tone, sing the lower.

(c) Play each of the intervals of (c) and determine whether it is a Major 2nd or Minor 7th, testing whether it is 4–5 or 5–4.

(2) Make exercises of absolute intervals as given in Lesson 25, Section B, page 141, and add the Major 2nd and Minor 7th.

(3) Practise the following intervals as outlined in the preceding lessons. The two dissonant intervals are used in section (b).

(4) Continue chord-practice of preceding lesson.

(5) *Melodies for Dictation and Singing;* Parallel construction, 3rd stage, and Contrasting construction, using melodic minor: and $\frac{4}{4}$ ♩. ♪　$\frac{6}{8}$ ♩ ♫

(a) In analysis of melodies, note the use of a figure in repetition and the sequence. In No. 1, measure 1, is a figure; measure 2 is a repetition of 1; measure 5 a repetition of 1, measure 6 a sequence of 5. Analysis of the use of figures is an invaluable aid to memorizing.

(b) After writing, mark figures, sequences and repetitions, as in example, Section A.

Section C.

(1) *Rhythmic Study:* ♩. ♪ in 2/4 and 3/4

In studying the ♩.♪ be sure that the sixteenth is felt as

the last of a group of four sixteenths ♫♫. not as a part of a

triplet

(2) *Exercises in Sight-Singing:*

CHAPTER XIX

Figure. Modified Repetition and Sequence

A figure can be used in *repetition* and *sequence* in *modified* forms.

A figure can be modified by

(1) Adding tones to the figure:

(2) Changing rhythm.
   (a) Dotting notes.

   (b) Contraction (making the note-values one-half as long).

   (c) Expansion (making the note-values twice as long).

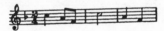

(3) Changing the size of the intervals.

(4) Using part of the figure in repetition and sequence.

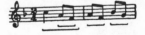

(5) By inversion, in exact or modified form.

LESSON 29

Section A.

(1) *Suggestions for Study:*

(a) Construct two Periods; one parallel, one contrasting, one major, one minor, in 4/4 and 6/8 meter: each antecedent phrase to have three consequent phrases.

Develop from a figure, one measure long, used in repetition and sequence, modified by adding tones and changing rhythm.

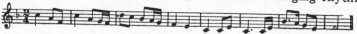

(b) Construct two periods as in (a). Develop from a figure one measure long, used in repetition and sequence, modified by adding tones, changing rhythm, and size of the intervals. Thus:

(c) Construct two periods, as in (a); develop as before using part of figure in sequence and repetition. Thus:

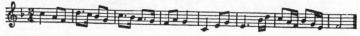

(d) Construct two periods, as in (a); develop as before, using the figure in inversion. Thus:

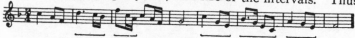

Section B.

(1) Continue practice of Absolute Intervals as outlined in Lesson 28, Section B, page 155.

(2) *Intervals for Practice* in the I and V⁷ chords.

(3) (a) Play the I–V⁷–I chords in every minor key.

(b) Sing these chords in arpeggio form using number and letter-names.

(4) *Melodies for Dictation and Singing.* Parallel and contrasting constructions. Figures in sequence and repetition, modified by adding tones and changing size of intervals.

(a) In melodic analysis determine figure first, then modifications.

(b) In outlining rhythm ♪♩ place 2 under dot and a check after, as this is the only figure of two uneven notes.

No. 3.

(c) After writing, mark figures, sequence and repetitions.

Section C.

(1) *Rhythmic Study:* ♪♩ in $\frac{4}{4}$

(2) *Exercises in Sight-Singing:*

CHAPTER XX

Period-Form (*continued*)

Parallel Construction by Sequence and Inversion

A period is in parallel construction when at least the first or the first two measures of the consequent phrase are a *sequence* of the antecedent phrase; it is then said to be *parallel by sequence*.

A period is in parallel construction when the first or the first two measures of the consequent phrase are an *inversion* of the antecedent phrase; it is then said to be *parallel by inversion*.

LESSON 30

Section A.

Suggestions for Study:

(1) Construct periods, making the consequent phrase a sequence of the antecedent. Thus:

(2) Construct periods, making the consequent phrase an inversion of the antecedent. Thus:

Section B.

(1) Continue practice of Absolute Intervals.

(2) *Intervals for Practice* in the I and V⁷ chords in minor.

    (a) Review Lesson 25, Section B (2), page 142.

    (b) Note the changed position of the Major and Minor 3rd and 6th in the I chord in minor. The intervals of the V⁷ in major and minor are the same.

(3) Continue chord-practice as outlined in the preceding lesson.

(4) *Melodies for Dictation and Singing.* Construction parallel, by sequence and inversion. Figures modified by adding notes, changing size of intervals, using dots and inversion.

Section C.

(1) *Rhythmic Study:* ♪ ♫♫ in 6/8

(2) *Exercises in Sight-Singing:*

CHAPTER XXI

Setting Words to Music

In setting words to music we shall begin with the common poetic form, the four-line stanza in trochaic tetrameter. The relation of this form to the phrase- and period-form in music is very close.

First scan the poem for long and short syllables; then find the number of long (or accented) syllables in the complete thought. Each long syllable will occupy an accented pulse in music.

The smallest form in music used to express a complete thought is a phrase.

The meter is determined by the number of long syllables in the complete thought of the poem. If there are four long syllables, the meter will be duple or triple; if eight, either a four- or a six-pulse meter.

The meter, whether duple or triple, is decided by the kind of feet used in the poem. A trochee (—◡) would be duple, a dactyl (—◡◡) triple. If the short syllable comes first, as in an iambus (◡—), the music will begin on the up-beat.

> "Twinkle, twinkle, little star,
> How I wonder what you are;
> Up above the world so high,
> Like a diamond in the sky."

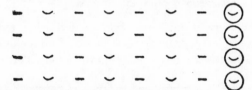

NOTE—Each line has a silent short syllable.

As this would be a compound sentence in prose, we use a Period in music. In the first phrase (two lines of the poem), there are eight long or accented syllables. Therefore we have either a four- or a six-pulse meter. At first sight we seem to require 4/4 meter, because of the constant trochaic rhythm. In reciting this poem we shall find that we really scan it —◡◡ with one silent short syllable. If this is the case, we shall use 6/8 meter. This seems the better, though either is possible.

The poem takes the following arrangement as to measure and phrase:

The melody will follow the melodic laws. The choice of high or low tones is determined from the importance of the words and syllables. The range will be from one to one and one-half octaves. In speaking the word *twinkle* the inflection on the first syllable is higher than on the second, so in our choice of tones we should select for the first syllable a tone higher in pitch than for the second. The most important word in the phrase is placed on the highest pitch. We might consider the climax of the phrase to be on *how wonder*, *what*, or *are*. *Wonder* is probably the best. In that case, *wonder* would receive the highest pitch. The choice of parallel or contrasting construction is optional.

Rhythmic variety may be obtained by using two or more pitches for one syllable, or by dotting notes. In those first attempts it is better to keep the rhythm as uniform as possible.

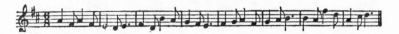

LESSON 31

Section A.

Suggestions for Study:

(1) Scan and outline rhythmically for musical setting, the following rhymes:

     Jack and Jill
     *Little Jack Horner
     *Little Miss Muffet
     *Mary, Mary
     Humpty Dumpty—

(2) Make musical settings of the poems.

(3) Use stanzas of your own choice or composition in the same meter.

Section B.

(1) Continue practice of Absolute Intervals.

(2) *Intervals for Practice* on I and V^7 chords, in minor.

(3) Continue chord-practice as in Lesson 29, Section B, page 162.

(4) *Melodies for Dictation and Singing.* All constructions and figure modifications are to be used.

*It will be found that in these rhymes the second line of each is lacking two syllables, and that in reciting we always wait for the time to pass that these syllables would occupy. For example, *Mary, Mary*, scans:

"Mary, Mary, quite contrary,
 How does your garden grow?
With silver bells and cockle shells
 And little maids all in a row."

NOTE. In outlining rhythm ♪♫♫ in **8** write 5 under the dot. No. 1

Section C.

(1) Review rhythmic drill of the preceding lesson.
(2) *Exercises in Sight-Singing:*